P

FOR COOKI
CLIMBING THE LADDER OF SUCCESS

"Have you been searching for a one-stop manual on how to get ahead in business and in life without getting caught up in second guessing and self doubt? If so, then Cookie Tuminello's *Climbing the Ladder of Success* is one of the 'must-have' books that you need to read to achieve your goals!"
– **Phyllis Granger, CEO, *Absolutely Irresistible Monogramming and Gifts* www.AI1313.com**

"What do you get when you mix one part common sense, then fill it with another part of success strategies, add a dash of spunk and spirit into the mix? Cookie Tuminello's book, *Climbing the Ladder of Success*, that's what! If you only read ONE book this year on how to advance your career and life, this is the one to get!"
– **Debbey Ryan, CEO, *Prescriptive Marketing* www.DebbeyRyan.com**

"I have had the good fortune to work with Cookie on several occasions and have always walked away from her presentations wanting more. I am so glad that's she's taken her wit and wisdom and put it all together in *Climbing the Ladder of Success*. Her book combines lessons that she teaches in her coaching practice along with practical steps that anyone can easily use to further their career. I am proud to say that Cookie is not only my mentor, she is my friend, and her book is just another great addition to her already overflowing toolbox of wonderful skill sets."
– **Lauralyn Maranto, Vice President of Administration and Human Resources, *Visit Baton Rouge* www.VisitBatonRouge.com**

"Thank you, Cookie, for sharing your life's lessons with us. You tell it like it is! Your book offers us steps to uncover our authentic self, our true passion and purpose for our lives, while your Action Exercises transform our goals into the success we only imagined. I was struggling to find peace among the chaos of my life. I had a demanding career, a young son, a ton of responsibilities to everyone and everything—least of all to myself—all of which kept me out of balance and out of energy. Cookie helped me discover my peace and recover the self that was lost. Her book is like a personal coaching course to uncover our true treasures. So, I say to anyone who wants to change the status quo, desires to shift chaos to peace, or to be the successful person that they aspire to be, keep this book handy! Apply Cookie's steps and work her Action Exercises, for she is offering you a very real way to reach the top of the ladder of success! I truly love this book and will buy copies for many, many friends! What Cookie created is a fantastic tool for transforming a life of chaos and mediocrity into one that is alive and kicking!"

– **Kathleen Abshire, COO, *Island Operating Company, Inc.*** **www.IslandOperating.com**

"Cookie's book, *Climbing the Ladder of Success,* helps you face your fears, and then gives you clear, concise action steps of how you can eliminate the roadblocks that are holding you back from being exactly who you want to be NOW. Not only is Cookie a fabulous coach, her practical way of 'saying it like it is' can accelerate your ambitions and catapult your career. Thanks Cookie!"

– **Linda Allred, *The Accelerated Results Weight Loss Expert*** **www.LindaAllred.com**

"If you are looking for a gentle reminder of how to be successful don't read this book. However, if you are ready to get to work, and start climbing the ladder of success, this book is for you. Funny,

direct, and honest, Cookie tells it like it is, giving guidance and support with 'no bull' advice on how to be successful while staying true to yourself. This book is packed with honest-to-goodness Southern wisdom right down to the lagniappes."
– **Dr. Rachelle Disbennett Lee, bestselling author of**
365 Days of Coaching **www.CoachLee.com**

"*Climbing the Ladder of Success* is a tell-it-like-it-is book. Cookie authentically recounts her own life story, revealing a powerful guide for self- actualization and success. She leads the reader to live from 'the inside out' in order to claim their power, find their voice, and make wise choices. She challenges the reader to move forward and chart a course for success. You will be inspired to action with every word."
– **Dr. Patricia Moore Harbour, CEO/President,**
Breakthrough Coaching and Harbour Center for Quality Education, LLC **www.MyBreakthroughCoach.com**

"It was many, many years after I got to the top of the ladder before I was content with myself. Cookie's words settle in my soul and provide freedom to sing when no one wanted to listen, dance when all alone, and live life like there is heaven on earth. I give thanks that women like Cookie came into my life for the second half. *Climbing the Ladder to Success* is a must read!"
– **Lou Patin, CEO, *King-Patin Limited* www.King-Patin.com**

"Through her book, Cookie Tuminello generously shows the way and teaches by example how anyone can succeed in business, especially in this new economy. This book is a must read for anyone who is serious about being a TRUE leader within their organization, their own business, or their own life. The book, like Cookie, is filled with an incredible depth of wisdom, passion, and of course, her signature Southern charm, that can have you laughing in one moment and feeling like you had a quick kick in your pants to get you MOVING up that ladder in the next.

Brilliant!"
– **Lynn Strigh, CEO, *Lynn Strigh International***
  www.LynnStrigh.com

"Cookie is that rare combination of bold and brave paired with kindness. She does more than inspire with her words; she is living proof that her methods equal success. And she does it all with a unique panache sure to leave a smile on your face and a bit more sass in your stride."
– **Amanda Bedgood, Editor, *FACE Magazine***
  www.FaceLafayette.com

"If you are true to yourself, the whole world benefits! In this sassy and sincere book, Cookie shares her amazing pearls of wisdom in a way that crystallizes just what that means. She walks her talk and gives you the permission to hold your head up high, move forward with gusto, and grab your personal power as you fast track to true freedom. If you are ready to leave the 'people-pleasing' to someone else and thrive, make sure to read this book cover to cover!"
– **Mariana Cooper (Mari), Host of the *Aha! Moments Radio Show* and founder of www.AhaMomentsInc.com**

"Here's the thing about Cookie's *Climbing the Ladder of Success*: It's not just a 'feel good' coaching program that makes you feel all warm and fuzzy inside, and it's not a program where you'll be buried in the same old tactics that make you feel like you're on a treadmill getting nowhere. Cookie has crafted a comprehensive business and leadership how-to read that cuts to the core of bringing the very best of YOU forward. And she does all this with her Southern charm that encourages yet challenges you every step of the way. If you're a business owner or leader who is ready to climb the ladder to success, then you'll want to read this book to gain the confidence, tools, and community you need to succeed."
– **Leslie Hamp, Certified Pilates and Lifestyle Coach bestselling author of *Create the Life You Crave***
  www.LeslieHamp.com

Climbing the Ladder of Success

Without Stepping on Your Values

COOKIE TUMINELLO

empowering teams and igniting productivity since 1999

TREMENDOUS
LIFE BOOKS.COM

Climbing The Ladder of Success Without Stepping on Your Values

Author: Cookie Tuminello

Book Editor: Marlene Oulton www.MarleneOulton.com

Portrait photo: Light Writer Photography

Book design: Roslyn Nelson

Cover design: Laurie Landry

The purpose of this book is to educate, enlighten, and inform persons seeking
personal and professional growth. It is sold with the understanding that neither
the author nor the publisher is engaged in rendering any psychological advice.
In instances where psychological or other professional opinions or advice
are appropriate, such professional counsel should be sought. The publisher
and author disclaim any liability whatsoever for an individual's use of any advice
or information presented within this book.

ISBN 978-1-936354-41-2

Dedication

TO MY COACHES AND MENTORS

*Thank you for inspiring me
to live my life with authenticity,
passion, purpose, and power
so that I could help others
to do the same.*

With Gratitude

There are some special people I want to thank for helping get this book out of my brain and into print for all of you to benefit from.

Marlene Oulton—editor, proofreader, copywriter extraordinaire, and friend; your ability to make words sing and dance is second to none. I am also honored that you penned a poem especially for this book. Thank you for your support and friendship.

Leslie Hamp—marketing and branding mentor; you are a powerhouse of creative ideas, strategies and inspiration for bold thinking.

Ros Nelson—publisher; thank you for taking care of details, keeping me focused, and helping to bring this book to life.

Clients, workshop participants, newsletter subscribers, and column readers; it has been a privilege to partner in your journey to success.

My colleagues; thank you for your friendship, support, honesty, and kick in the butt when I needed it.

Friends and family who have been there for me in the good, not so good, and sad times; thank you for being the anchor I could always hold onto when the going got rough. Thank you for listening to me time and time again when I whined and lamented while working on this book, "Sorry, I can't go this weekend. I have to work on my book."

And last, but certainly not least, to my children, Gina, Deuce (Frank II); daughter-in-law, Heather; son-in-law, Brad; and eight beautiful grandchildren: Brady and Zachary (twins), Emily, Isabella, Trey (Frank, III), Ella Kate. I thank God every day for the blessings and contributions you make to me in my life.

My love to all of you,

Cookie

Cookie Tuminello

TABLE OF CONTENTS

HOW TO READ AND USE THIS BOOK

First of all, this book is about helping you work *smarter* not *harder*. I'd like to share a couple of recommendations with you about how to digest all the information you're about to read in this book and give you a few pointers on how to process it to your advantage.

I strongly suggest that you read this book in its entirety without taking any action the first time around so that you can let it all sink in. It contains a lot of "brain food" and while you most likely will be very excited to start making changes in your life *now*, it's important to see the whole picture before taking action. I sincerely don't want you to become overwhelmed or feel as if you're heading in the wrong direction due to lack of instructions.

Once you've read the complete book, go back to the beginning and do each Action Exercise, step-by-step, until you've finished working them all. Don't skip any steps! Even if you feel you are ready to skip a step, each of them has a specific place in my plan to save you time and effort, while helping you gain self-confidence, as well as not having to reinvent the wheel to get moving and see results.

Remember: take this whole process slowly. Reading and absorbing all the steps in this book is not a race against time. Digest each one carefully and completely before moving on to the next step. Treat it like you would eat an elephant—one bite at a time.

The key is to just make up your mind to do the work. I imagine that a lot of you have read books that you thought were so amazingly great that you underlined passages and highlighted sections so that you could go back and easily find them when you needed a gentle reminder of what you learned. I'd also bet that at least once in your life you put that book right back on a shelf in your bookcase and never applied all the great ideas you read about. Well, the last thing I want to see happen is that you put this book back up on your bookshelf to collect dust along with a ton of other how-to or self-help books. Your career, life, *and* money are too important to waste!

Commit to completing these lessons. Please know that there is no such thing as a quick fix for any given set of challenges. You actually have to do the work for the principles of this book to manifest themselves into your life. Just take the time, make a commitment, and take it one section a day until you've completed the book and action steps to manifest change into your life.

About the Lagniappe

After every chapter you will find a section called Lagniappe. If you are not from the deep South (primarily Louisiana and Mississippi), in all probability you have not ever heard this word before. When my editor saw it, her first comment was, "Is this a typo? I've never seen this word before." Let me explain.

Lagniappe is a Southern colloquialism meaning something given or obtained as a gratuity or bonus. Pronounced "**lan**-yap," it is a small gift that you did not expect. So, after each chapter there will be a little something extra (lagniappe) to further your learning and give you food for thought. Enjoy!

INTRODUCTION

"If we don't change, we don't grow.
If we don't grow, we are not really living.
Growth demands a temporary surrender of security."

~ Gail Sheehy

There is no doubt about it. The winds of change are upon us. The degree to which you succeed in your life, business, or career will be your willingness and ability to adapt to change.

The marketplace is changing and so are the dynamics of what it means to be a business leader in the world today. We are entering what is known as the conceptual era. This new leadership paradigm, or leader shift, will require not only tech-savvy skills, but soft skills as well to create long-term, sustainable results. The good news is that most of us already possess these innate skills.

The problem is that we have been trying to live our lives and do business according to other people's standards and expectations, which has left us frustrated, exhausted, and unfulfilled. It has even caused us to sabotage our own success because we are constantly trying to think, act, and feel in a way that is in total contradiction with our own authenticity, integrity, and core values.

Here are just a few of the ways that I and many others have sabotaged ourselves in our personal and professional lives.

◆ We are afraid to ask for what we really want.

◆ We often use excuses, usually involving money and time, for not taking advantage of opportunities that are right in front of us.

◆ We allow fear of rejection and failure to get in the way of taking action.

◆ We don't always have enough confidence in ourselves so we hold back.

- We allow other people's expectations of ourselves to determine our own actions.

- We are afraid to raise our fees because some of our clients might leave.

- We settle for less than what we really want and accept the status quo because we feel as though we don't have any other choices.

More good news—you're not alone!

If you're like most professional, successful people, you're very good at what you do, but have a difficult time setting boundaries, saying no, asking for what you want, handling difficult conversations, carving out *me time*, and instead, come from a place of people-pleasing. This has created havoc in your personal and your professional life, and sometimes you have felt like you were powerless to change.

Before we go any further, let me put your mind at ease about one thing. **There is nothing wrong with you!** You do have the power to change things. All the power you need is right inside of you waiting to be tapped. You just need a *personal power tune-up* to get your engines running at maximum capacity.

How many times have you wondered if there was someone who could finally show you the steps to working smarter, without having to push so hard all the time?

There is someone who can help you and that someone would be me. Having been there, done that, got the T-shirt, I know what it's like to feel frustrated and lack the support and encouragement to pursue one's dreams. I know what it's like to have money and business opportunities slip through my hot little hands because I was too afraid to take advantage of them.

The strategies and tools in this book were designed to help people just like *you*—people who want to be more in control of their lives.

It all boils down to one thing. Do you want to live a life that is mired in mediocrity and struggle or do you want to live a life filled with passion, purpose, love, joy, prosperity, and success beyond your wildest dreams? The choice is yours. Choose wisely.

So, get on the ladder of success—and let the transformation process begin!

STEP ONE:
DEFINING WHAT SUCCESS MEANS TO YOU

*"All my life I wanted to be somebody, but I see now
I should have been more specific."*

– Jane Wagner

I just love that quote by Jane Wagner, as it describes how most of my clients feel when they first come to me for help. They know something isn't working in their life and/or business, and they're fairly certain that they're not as happy or successful as they want to be, but they haven't figured out how to invite that state of happiness back into their life. Frankly, they're still trying to figure out who that *somebody* is in the big picture. When I ask them, "Who is *somebody* and what does that look like to you?" I usually get a blank stare back until they get their "Aha!" moment and are able to answer me. I also refer to this as one of those "Wake up, Alice—this ain't Wonderland" moments in my coaching practice.

Let me give you an example. When I first started coaching, you could say that I was in Wonderland because I just wanted to help people to be successful. Right! That was about as clear as mud. It's no wonder it took me so long to get where I was going. And yes, there were times when I would whine because I didn't get what I wanted. Imagine that. Thank goodness I had an excellent coach and mentor who taught me that if I wanted to get somewhere in my life I was going to have to get a lot more specific about the details. What I learned was that I could not get where I wanted to go by asking the same questions I had been asking. I needed to start asking new ones.

Let's get serious about this. This is your life we're talking about here. If you don't get clear about where you're going, how are you going to get there? You wouldn't get in your car and aimlessly take any old exit ramp on the freeway hoping that you'll end up at your destination would you? No? I didn't think so.

The way I see it you have two choices. You can choose to be an active participant in your life, or you can choose to be an unconscious observer, swept along by the passage of time. Here's what I mean by that. Most of the time we sit around wishing and waiting for others to change so we can have what we want. Well, guess what—the only person you can change is yourself. Sounds like a no-brainer to me.

Before you go a step further, you need to stop and think about where your life is right now. Are you where you want to be in this moment? If you're not, then what action or addition to your life would make an immediate difference right now? Could it be more fun, more success, more business, more money, more balance, family time, travel, or maybe a home on the beach? You can't go somewhere when you don't have directions. Would you leave on a vacation without directions or a map? I think not. So why would you run your life like that? This first Action Exercise will help you to determine that.

Success is not a one-size-fits-all type of deal. It is different for everyone. And the degree to which you determine what it looks like to you, the more passion, purpose, and fulfillment you'll experience.

The **Wake Up, Alice, This Is Your Life** Action Exercise 1 on the next page will certainly help you to delve deeper into finding out where you are, where you want to go, and what areas of your life need adjusting so that you can live a more harmonious and fulfilled life with a lot less stress and regret.

▶ Action Exercise 1
"WAKE UP ALICE, THIS IS YOUR LIFE"

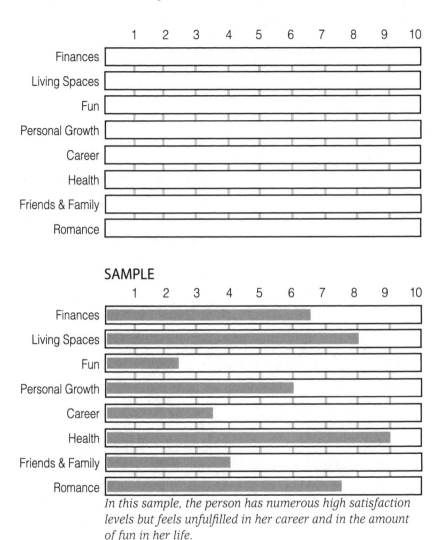

In this sample, the person has numerous high satisfaction levels but feels unfulfilled in her career and in the amount of fun in her life.

How to chart your satisfaction

◆ The eight sections in our "This is Your Life" chart represent all the domains (areas) of your life. From left to right, rate your degree of satisfaction with each domain by filling in an amount (0 to 10) that represents how successful each area feels to you. The goal is not necessarily to have all "tens" but to see if there is a reasonable balance between the areas.

◆ Next, ask yourself, "What changes do I want to make to increase my level of satisfaction?" Do this for each life area. Write down one answer for each section that will significantly alter the quality of your life.

◆ Commit to taking some action right now!

Here's an example of what I did at the beginning of this year to bring more fulfillment and well-being into my life. After looking over the numbers on my own chart, I realized that one of the domains that I wanted to focus on was my health. My intention when doing the chart is always to bring my level of satisfaction up a notch whenever possible. I think this is where a lot of us sabotage our results because we want to go from zero to 10 at mach speed and when it doesn't happen we get frustrated and quit. Remember it's PACE, not RACE. Consistency is the key to change.

The health section was a biggie for me. I had gained 20 pounds since I moved here to Lafayette a few years ago, and I had not participated in any exercise regimen since my knee surgery which also took place three years ago. So, for me the action step was to find a workout routine that I liked and would stick with. And I did find it. I absolutely love my Pilates Proformer™ machine full-body workouts. It makes me feel so empowered. I consistently go to three classes a week. After three months I am proud to say that I have lost two inches off my waist and hips. In addition, I wanted to find a weight-loss program with a good nutritional basis that I could sustain consistently—not just for a few months and a few less pounds. I wanted something that allowed me to have all the foods I liked but in moderation, so I joined Weight Watchers®. After three months, I have also lost 13 pounds and couldn't feel better. So, where am I in terms of level of satisfaction? I am very satisfied with my consistency, progress, and results. *You must remember that creating satisfaction and fulfillment in your life is what you believe it to be, not what others think it should be.* And that is where you will find peace and fulfillment in your life. Now that you've taken a look at where you are and rated your level of satisfaction in all areas of the chart, this next Action Exercise will help you become even clearer about where you want to go. It will also help you identify what fears may be keeping you stuck so that you can determine if they are real or just a story you've been telling yourself.

▶ Action Exercise 2
DEFINING WHAT SUCCESS LOOKS LIKE TO YOU

This Action Exercise will help you get a clearer picture of where you want to go. It will help you separate the real deal from the fictional part of the messages you've been telling yourself for years.

◆ What's most important to you in your life?

◆ What's working in your life?

◆ What's not working in your life?

◆ What would you like to have more of in your life?

◆ What would you like to have less of in your life?

◆ What is one change you could make that would make an immediate difference in your life right now?

◆ What are the fears that have kept you from making this change in the past?

◆ How would you feel (in vivid detail) if you were to make this change in your life?

◆ What would be the positive results you would enjoy if you made this change?

Making your visions of success a reality

Once you complete the first two Action Exercises of Step One, you'll have a clearer picture of where you're going and what success looks like to you. So, before you can take the first step toward whatever your vision of success would look like to you, you need to write down your definitions on paper, and not leave them aimlessly floating around in your mind.

What is the "more" that you're looking for? What is the feeling that you're looking for? How will you recognize it when you see it? One of the best resources I can recommend that you use is Henriette Klauser's book, *Write It Down, Make It Happen.* This is one of the best books that I have ever read that explains and reinforces the necessity of writing down what you want to accomplish in your life.

When I started reading Henriette's book, flashbulbs started going off in my head left and right. Up until that time I thought I had a very good system for achieving my goals—I kept them in my head. Being the private person that I was at the time and not open to a lot of vulnerability, I thought that was a good place to keep things. Well, it's a good place if you want to hide them, but not a good one if you want to achieve them. When you keep your desires buried firmly in your mind, you leave yourself an escape hatch—a back door, if you will—to be out of integrity with yourself. I left that back door open for a lot of years, and I also used that back door to sabotage myself. I also thought that if I kept them in my head and failed to achieve those goals, then I would not have to suffer the embarrassment of failure.

Keep the list where you can easily see it every day. It makes it more real.

When I say I view them every day, I do mean every single day. That old saying, "Out of sight, out of mind" definitely holds true in this scenario. If you can't see your goals, you can't achieve them. Keeping them in front of you at all times is what's going to keep you honest and accountable to yourself. Otherwise, all those people pleaser habits take over and you wind up taking care of everything and everybody but YOU.

When I first started this practice, I would write down my intentions daily and I still do. Then one day my own personal coach reminded me that if I wanted to succeed, I had to not only write them down, I had to **1)** keep them where I could see them, and **2)** read them in the morning when I got up and again at night before going to bed. Imagine what a thump on the head that was for me, but my coach was right. By revisiting my intentions twice daily I was able to stay focused, accountable, and moving forward. I also closed that back door and quit looking back. I think that the most important aspect of writing down my intentions daily is that it kept me from getting sidetracked with things that were not important, or not in keeping with where I truly wanted to go. You know, those bright, shiny objects that show up just to distract us, but send us off on tangents that can totally derail our intentions.

▶ Action Exercise 3
MAKING YOUR INTENTIONS (GOALS) A REALITY

Here's what I do now to keep myself on track and accountable.

◆ I write down my goals on 3 x 5 index cards and keep them in my journal where I can read them in the morning and evening.

◆ Since I am a visual person, I relate strongly to pictures, so in addition to my 3 x 5 cards, I create a **Vision Board** for myself annually.

Here's how I do this Action Exercise. I take an 11x14 piece of poster board and I cut pictures out of magazines that remind me of my visions (intentions), which I then paste onto my poster board. I paint a picture of what I want to create that year and then tack my Vision Board on my bulletin board in my office in plain sight. That way I keep my goals right in front of me. Every time I look up from my computer, there they are. This works for me and I know it will work for you as well.

Let me share with you an example of how I manifested one of my intentions.

"I'm going to Italy next year."

One of my intentions for 2004 was to go to Italy, as it had always been my dream to visit the land of my ancestors. I didn't have the money to travel abroad at the time, but I knew in my heart that at some point I was going to Italy. I went to a local travel agency, told them about my dream vacation spot, how long I wanted to stay, and what cities I wanted to visit. I was then informed that if I enrolled 20 people for this excursion, my trip would be paid for. Every single day I would look up at my Vision Board, gaze at the pictures of the towns I wanted to visit, and just daydream I was walking through that town. I announced my trip in my newsletter and invited folks to join me on "Cookie's Great Italy Tour." I hosted a wine and cheese get together at my home and friends brought friends. And so the journey began.

Did I experience some setbacks? Sure I did. First there was a crisis that broke out in Europe which caused everyone to rethink the trip. Then we had to postpone it until the spring because we did not have enough folks opt in. I was determined that none of these events was going to stop me from going to Italy. Every day I came into my office, turned on my computer, looked up, and the first thing I saw was my pictures of all the places and things I was going to see when I went to Italy. I could literally feel myself there and the excitement of that vision kept me smiling all day. I also kept saying to myself, "I just can't wait to be in Italy." It did not matter that the trip was postponed; I knew I was going and spoke aloud this belief every day. In the end destiny prevailed and the trip became a reality.

In March of 2005, myself and 19 other fun-loving folks boarded a plane for Italy and I was the tour director. You have to believe in the power of your dreams and speak about them as if they've already happened in your life. So, go ahead! Dream big! The achievement of your goals is only hampered by the degree to which you believe they WON'T happen, which brings me to one of the most important keys to success, namely your mindset!

Mindset is everything!

Success is a mindset. Your thoughts, feelings, and actions must be in sync to create the results you want in your life. If your inside thoughts don't match your outside behavior, you are in a world of trouble.

Your thoughts, feelings, and actions are determined by your beliefs. Your beliefs are a direct result of your history—what you have been taught or experienced during your childhood. For example, I was brought up hearing and believing from my mother that success was really, really, hard work, and you had to really, really struggle to get there. I also had the belief that because I didn't graduate from college, that I wasn't smart enough to be successful. Well, guess what? I manifested just that: hard work, lots of struggle, and feelings of inadequacy. It wasn't until I began to dissect and challenge those old beliefs that my life and my business began to change.

Most of the fears and beliefs that we hold as true are not. They are stories (illusions) that we tell ourselves when no one else is around. They are the "yeah, buts" and the "what ifs" that are whispered down deep in our soul where we know no one can hear them.

You can read affirmations and feel-good books all day long, but until you evict those old beliefs that no longer serve you, from your mind and body, you will never be FREE. You will never receive the abundance and success you deserve in your life. To this day I am still ejecting outdated beliefs out of my mind. However, the one thing that has changed is that I have shortened my response time and I don't allow them to keep me stuck. I now have the tools to move through them faster. In order to succeed you must know three things:

◆ Where you are,

◆ Where you are going, and

◆ Why are you going.

Most of us would say right away, "Well, I know that!" *But do you really, really, really know what you want, where you are going, or what your purpose is in your life?*

The difference between what you say you know is what you do, and what you do controls your results. If what you are doing is not producing the results you want then you really don't know where you want to end up, do you?

The first key to unlocking your success is knowing where you are right now. As I stated earlier, this requires that you start asking questions that you may not have been asking before. It's about going back through your life and picking up the pieces of yourself that you have left behind one by one. For example, are the actions you are presently taking what you really want, or have they been adopted from someone else's statement of what you should be doing? If the choices you've made are not in alignment with your core values, you might want to rethink where you are in your life today.

Second, you also need to know where you are going. How are you going to get where you're going if you don't know where your final destination is? Better yet, how are you going to lead others if you aren't clear about what your goal is?

Third, you have to ask why are you going there. What's your purpose? Do you have one? Are you 100% committed to where you are going? You have to get clear about what is driving you.

My clients tell me all the time, "Cookie, you sure ask a lot of different questions that I never thought of before." And I reply, yes I do ask a lot of questions, but they're designed to make you really think intentionally about what you want and what you want "it" to look like when you get there. When you begin to think differently, you begin to get better results. And you don't have as much disappointment or second guessing when you get there.

Like I said in the beginning, mindset is key to getting where you want to go. You must be in the right mindset to take the right steps. You must open your mind and your heart. Success means being open to new ideas, possibilities, and learning; simply put, being open to change.

Even though we say we want to change, it's hard stepping out of our cushy comfort zone. That first step can be pretty scary. Fear will always pop up when you are in unfamiliar territory. Just remember—when those negative voices inside of you say, "No way am I doing that!" just thank that little voice for sharing and tell it to go away. Believe that you can do whatever you choose to do and move on.

Change involves making choices and taking risks. You can't get where you want to go if you're not open to new ideas and new possibilities. Success comes to those who are willing to make the choice and take the risk. If you have a closed mind and are unwilling to look at different ways of doing things, the chances of you succeeding at anything are greatly diminished. Had I not been open to new ideas, I would not have been able to go to Italy.

Here's something for you to think about when the fear creeps in and tries to hold you back.

Only you can control your future and your destiny

You may think that others control your future, but they don't. Your choices brought you to where you are in your life, be they good, bad, or ugly. And if you don't like where you are, then it is up to you to change this fact.

If you are ready to make this year your best year ever, then you are going to have to take a stand for YOU. Nobody is going to automatically give you the things you desire the most. Whether you are a business owner or organizational leader, nobody is going to take you seriously if you don't take yourself seriously.

The sooner you start working on kicking your old habits that are no longer working out the door, the better your life is going to be. The havoc of being caught up in this never-ending cycle of pleasing everyone but yourself wears you down, both mentally and physically. I know. I've been there.

So, where do you want to be at the end of this year? Did you make New Year's resolutions or did you make commitments? Making resolutions just doesn't cut it for me because they always feel like *shoulds* instead of *choices*. I prefer to set intentions and make commitments for my new year, because when I do I'm more committed to making them happen. I then write it down in my journal so it makes it real to me. My intention this year is to make it the best year ever. I get excited just talking about it.

So, how do you make this happen? You plan for it. Here are the steps that have worked for me and I know they will work for you, too.

I determine where I want to be at the end of the year. What does that look like? How is it going to feel when I get there? I then create my vision of how the year is going to unfold. For example, this year my intention is to double my business.

▶ Action Exercise 4
HOW DO I ACHIEVE MY GOALS?

Here are questions I ask which help me in achieving my goals.

◆ What is that going to look like in dollars? More clients? More subscribers? Additional products? Double my speaking engagements? Develop a marketing plan?

◆ Is my vision in keeping with my core values? Core values are what keep me aligned with my integrity so I don't second guess myself.

◆ What's working and what's not working in my business? What do I need to change to make it work better?

- What are the action steps that I need to take to get to this next level of success?

- What is the time frame for my action steps?

- What kind of support will I need to make it happen? What requests will I need to make?

- What are the obstacles that get in my way and hold me back? How will I handle them and move through them?

- How will I feel a year from now if nothing has changed and I have taken no action?

- How will I feel when I achieve my vision? (I can tell you right now, I would be beside myself with joy.)

- How will I reward myself when I achieve my vision?

Remember: Waiting on others to determine your fate is a dead end street. The only way to have a future that you want and will embrace when you get it is to design it yourself. Then you have less regret and more success.

ONLY YOU HAVE THE POWER TO CHANGE YOUR LIFE

"And the trouble is,
if you don't risk anything,
you risk even more."

– Erica Jong

How many of you whine and moan about what's not working in your businesses/life, but don't take the necessary action to change your present circumstances? Given the responses I get from participants in my workshops, there are quite a few of you.

How many times do you hear yourself making these comments?

- I wish I made more money.

- I wish I had more clients.

- I wish I had more time.

- I wish I didn't have to work so hard.

Sound familiar? To quote one of my favorite sayings, *"Wake up, Alice. This ain't Wonderland!"* Wishing and hoping for things to change in your business or personal life is not going to cut it. The *Good Change Fairy* is not going to come and sprinkle pixie dust on you and miraculously make everything in your life all better.

You can attend all the success workshops in the world, (including mine), read all the success and motivational books you can get your hands on, but *until you take action, nothing will change.* I'm not talking about just any action, but focused, inspired action.

You can't expect to achieve new goals by doing the same things you've been doing. It doesn't work like that. You have to set the stage and create the environment for change to take place. If you want to move beyond your present circumstances, it is going to take three things: support, accountability, and focused-inspired action.

SUPPORT—Why is support so important? If you could have done it on your own, you would have made the necessary changes already. Whether you choose a mentor or a coach, support is critical to your success. For example, I am pretty driven, but I know for a fact that had I not had the support of my coaches, I would not have made the strides I've made in my business or my life. Having the right kind of support challenges you to think bigger about yourself. Challenges make you take bigger, bolder action, and ultimately catapult you to your next level of success. This is what I mean by creating the environment for success to take place.

ACCOUNTABILITY—Why is accountability so important? Again, if you could have done it on your own, you would have done it already. For example, I had a goal to complete my book by the fall of this year. Could I have done it on my own? Sure I could, but if I didn't have my coach and my copy editor keeping me accountable every week and holding me to my intentions, I would procrastinate and make excuses. Accountability keeps you from sabotaging yourself. Been there, done that, got the T-shirt.

FOCUSED, INSPIRED ACTION—Why focused, inspired action? There is a difference between being busy and taking inspired action. In order to take inspired action, you must first have a clear vision of what form your goal or intention takes. If you don't know where you are going then you can't get there, and you certainly can't motivate others to follow you. Most people are really busy day in and day out, but are you busy doing the things that matter most or are you just putting out fires all day long?

I have a statement taped on my wall above my computer that says, **"Is what I'm working on right now getting me closer to my goal? If not, stop doing it immediately."**

The bottom line here is this: I know you know all these steps, but the big question is are you taking action? If you don't like your present circumstances, then change what you're doing.

STEP TWO:
USING YOUR CORE VALUES TO MAKE ALL YOUR DECISIONS

"The difference between success and merely surviving is the ability to discover and recognize your own core capabilities, then integrate them into every aspect of your personal and professional life."

– Charlie Bloom

Now that you have defined what it is that you want more of in your life, let's move on to what's next—defining your core values.

Just what are core values? Do you know what yours are? Most people may know what they are on an unconscious level, but on a conscious level they would have trouble describing them if they had never done a core values exercise.

For example, when I ask clients what their core values are, most will respond by saying that they treat people the way they want to be treated, or by describing how they care for their family, or how they express their faith. But then, when I ask them how these values are showing up in their life and influencing their decisions, it takes them a while to define for me what is really happening, day-by-day.

The same holds true when I work with organizational teams. I always want to look at their mission statements and core values to see if and how they are showing up in the overall actions and intentions of the team. You can easily tell when values and actions are not in alignment because it causes disconnectedness and ineffective practices.

With that being said, *core values are who you are, not who you think you are, should be, need to be, or want to be.* They are woven into the intricate fabric of your life. Core values help you make better decisions for yourself by keeping you true to what matters most in your life.

The difference between success and merely surviving is the ability to define and recognize your core values, then integrate them into every aspect of your personal and professional life. Core values are the foundation for creating the life you want and deserve. They must be present in everything you do in order for you to feel truly at peace with yourself. Let me offer an example of how this might show up in your life.

How many of your life choices reflect your core values?

Out of all of the everyday decisions you make, how many would you say are *shoulds* and how many are *choices?* For instance, how many times have you made a decision and two minutes later you regretted making it? In all probability you made a decision that was not in alignment with your core values, so consequently you made the wrong choice for yourself. You most likely made that choice to please someone else, and you were probably resentful about it as well. This is what happens when you make choices for yourself that are not based on your core values.

You've probably heard the phrase, "If it feels right to you, do it." There is some validity to that saying. If you feel uncomfortable doing something, this is because of the struggle between your core values and your decision. Some people call it your conscience talking to you, telling you that you've made a wrong move, and they're partially right. I also believe it's your core values sending you a clear message that the decision you've just made is going to have a negative impact on your life, and that you'd better change it now before the snowball starts rolling down the slope and it's too late to stop it.

When you base all your decisions on your core values, you never have to second guess yourself again. You will always be in integrity with yourself.

The following Action Exercise is a very powerful one for my clients because when they complete it, they see decision making as a much more conscious process. This exercise also helps them to make more informed, responsible, and accountable decisions. It sets the tone and foundation for what they want in their life. My clients tell me that out of all the Action Exercises that I do with them, this one is the most impactful and creates the biggest shift in their reality.

▶ Action Exercise 5
CORE VALUES—PART ONE

Right now take some quiet time, sit down with a piece of paper and pen, and ask yourself these questions.

◆ What was the most memorable and happiest event in your life (child, adult, personal or professional) that stands out in your memory?

◆ What was it about that event that made it so special?

◆ What did that moment feel like? For example, did you feel free, accepted, accomplished, valued, loved, acknowledged, secure, empowered?

◆ What do I value most in my life right now?

◆ When am I happiest in my life?

In this Action Exercise, I usually ask my clients to remember the happiest time in their life, but not everyone has had a lot of happy moments. With that being said, I want to share this story with you.

A few years back I facilitated a *Life Skills* training program for a nonprofit organization that provided a transitional housing program for unaccompanied, homeless women. The intention of this training program was to support the women in moving forward with their lives, developing life management skills, and self-confidence.

The problem with doing this Action Exercise with this particular group was that some of these women could not recall a happy time in their lives. Some of them had been physically or sexually abused, were recovering from alcohol or drug abuse (or both) and had been incarcerated at some point in their lives. Some had not even had the basic necessities of life while growing up. For some of the participants in this group, the Action Exercise was about recalling the worst time in their life, a time when they felt intimidated, worthless, fearful, abused, or used. Out of that experience, these women were able to define what they did not want in their life anymore. After completing this Action Exercise, they now had the tools to make better life choices for themselves.

To this day, my work with this group of women was one of the most rewarding and humbling experiences of my career. From this experience I learned trust, vulnerability, and compassion. I am grateful and honored to have been a part of it.

What is most important to note here is that no matter what your past life experiences are, you can use your core values as a guide to make better life choices for yourself.

Your answers to the questions in Action Exercise 5 have probably jogged your thought processes and created some clarity on how you want to "show up in your life." Now it is time to do PART TWO of the Core Values Action Exercise.

CORE VALUES—PART TWO: A WORKSHEET

Freedom	Achievement	Intelligence
Health	Friendship	Happiness
Adventure	Communication	Respect
Personal Development	Security	Authenticity
Family Connection	Integrity	Excitement
Beauty	Fun (Play)	Humor
Fulfillment	Wealth	Success
Recognition	Power	Passion
Spiritual Connection	Challenge	Love
Intimacy	Confidence	Personal Power
Inner Harmony	Success	Creativity
Contribution (Making a Difference)	Independence	

The words above are those most often used to define what makes up our own personal core values. Core values are who we are right now, not who we think we should be somewhere down the road. They help you define what matters most to you in life and are the basis for making better choices for yourself. They are the foundation for creating the life you want and deserve.

Go through the Action Exercise 5 list and pick out what you believe are your top 10 values. Next, go through your top 10 values list and pick out the top five values that really speak to you and write them in the second column. While all of your values are important to you, these five will be the ones that you know deep within your heart *must* be present in order to feel truly at peace with yourself.

When you have selected the top five values, take a look at where you are in your life right now and how closely your current choices reflect those values. This may be a bit uncomfortable as you will notice that some of your choices in life have pulled you away from your values. That's okay, because this Action Exercise is all about awareness. The good news is, now that you have this new awareness, you can use this information to make positive changes toward creating your own authenticity.

TOP 10 CORE VALUES LIST

1. _____

2. _____

3. _____

4. _____

5. _____

6. _____

7. _____

8. _____

9. _____

10. _____

TOP 5 CORE VALUES LIST

1. _____

2. _____

3. _____

4. _____

5. _____

Now, ask yourself the following questions to further align your core values with your actions.

◆ How are these core values showing up or not showing up in my life?

◆ What do I need to change to be in alignment with my core values?

◆ Who do I need to become to have the life I want and deserve?

Once you have completed the Action Exercise and defined what your core values are, here's what I would like for you to do next.

Write your top five core values on a 3 x 5 index card. Keep this card in a prominent place (on your desk or day planner), where you can see it at all times. That way every time you have to make a decision or choice, you can check in with yourself to make sure your decision is in alignment with your core values. If your decision is in alignment with your core values, you will feel a sense of integrity deep within yourself.

Before you make decisions always ask yourself, "What do I really want to do?" Then stop long enough to listen to what your gut (or core values) is telling you.

The majority of the time, I would be willing to bet that you didn't even ask yourself this question before making a decision because you were too busy trying to please everybody else. The reason I know this for a fact is that I used to do the same thing before I learned strategies that help me take better care of myself, and these same strategies, included in this book, will do the same for you.

By taking a few minutes and asking yourself this simple question, "What do I want?" your gut or core values will send you a clear answer on how to proceed. If you hear a resounding *no,* immediately stop and rethink what you are about to do. Better to put the brakes on now before you start down a new path than to have to go back later and correct your mistakes.

Now, using your **Top Five Core Values List** as your foundation, go back and take a look at your definition of success in Action Exercise 5 in Step One. Does your definition of success reflect who you are (core values) and what matters most in your life? If not, you might want to rethink your choices.

I think it is important to bring up a question about core values that my clients ask me all the time. That question is, "Do your core values change?" My answer to that question is this: yes, they change as you grow and become more conscious about what is most important in your life. For example, one of my core values has always been freedom. In the beginning of my journey of change, I didn't know how to define it any other way but to be free from other people's boundaries and expectations of what I should or should not be or do. As I grew and learned more about myself, I found that now my core value of freedom has deepened and expanded to be the freedom to express myself, freedom to be me, freedom to choose, to connect, and to be open and vulnerable.

Determine what's working and not working in your life. Focus solely on what's working and get rid of the rest.

Now that you're getting clearer about what you want, where you're going, and your core values, you will have a better sense about how to determine what's working and not working in your life. For instance, what are you merely tolerating? Could it be a job you don't like, a friend you don't care for that much, a chore you're not fond of doing, going to meetings you dislike, not speaking up in meetings, saying *yes* when you want to say *no*, procrastinating on a room that needs painting, fixing a broken faucet, or being in a relationship that isn't fulfilling? Whatever it is, you do have a choice about what you want and don't want in your life. Being a victim of these tolerations does not serve you well, and as long as there are incomplete and unfinished items in your life, you can't move on to bigger and better things. Remember—you decide whether you want to be the victim or victor. It's up to you! This next Action Exercise will help you take a look at what's working and not working in your life.

▶ *Action Exercise 6*

WHAT'S WORKING, WHAT'S NOT WORKING IN YOUR LIFE

As you can see, the next page is divided into two columns. To the left of the page is the column for "What's Working" and to the right is one for "What's Not Working" in your life. Now start making your lists. Just write down as many items as you can think of right now. Don't worry about running out of room. You probably have lots of additional paper on hand that you can use to do this Action Exercise if need be. Then, by the side of the "What's Not Working" item, place a date by which to complete it or to get rid of the toleration. My motto is *Do it, delegate it, or dump it.* Remember to start off small. Get rid of the little things first and work your way up to the big things. You will be amazed at how much space those tolerations take up in your life.

Below is an example of some of the items I put on my list when I did this exercise.

◆ **What's working in my life:** great career; loving relationships; cherished friends; wonderful family; terrific living environment—love where I live.

◆ **What's not working in my life:** Procrastination about taking car into shop for service; scheduling too many out-of-office appointments every day; not enough time spent in my office working on business development or projects.

Here are the action steps I took to get rid of some of what was not working on my list.

◆ Set up a time and date to take the car in for service.

◆ Having to be out at meetings all day, everyday is one of my pet peeves. It tears down my productivity and effectiveness. In an effort not to sabotage myself, I set what I call business development days. Monday and Friday are days when I don't schedule out-of-office appointments. Monday is for preparation and Friday is a wind-down day when I handle tasks not completed during the week such as emails or phone calls. I'm more organized, productive, effective, and definitely less frustrated.

Now it is your turn to list and get rid of what you're tolerating in your life. Assign a date to *do it, delegate it or dump it!*

WHAT'S WORKING IN YOUR LIFE

WHAT'S NOT WORKING IN YOUR LIFE

_____ _____

_____ _____

_____ _____

_____ _____

_____ _____

_____ _____

_____ _____DATE:_____

_____ _____

_____ _____

_____ _____

_____ _____

_____ _____

_____ _____DATE:_____

_____ _____

_____ _____

_____ _____

_____ _____

_____ _____

_____ _____DATE:_____

_____ _____

_____ _____

_____ _____

_____ _____

_____ _____

_____ _____DATE:_____

Remember that when you quit procrastinating and start taking action to get rid of these pesky little tolerations in your life, you start making room for the big things you want to accomplish. I don't know about you, but I feel better just writing down the things I want to happen and then getting rid of the things I'm tolerating to please someone else.

SIX QUESTIONS TO ASK BEFORE YOU MAKE A HASTY DECISION!

"Look twice before you leap."

– Charlotte Brontë

Weathering these challenging times is causing some professionals to make desperate decisions that are not in the best interest of their business or their life.

When you make desperate decisions you create desperate results. What do I mean by this? It's like putting a Band Aid on a gunshot wound. It's a short-term and ill-advised solution. When you make decisions out of desperation, you are reacting as opposed to responding to the situation, which in some cases can do more harm than good. The bottom line is that when you make these decisions you are not honoring you or your company's core values.

These desperate decisions can show up as taking on clients you wouldn't normally do business with or drastically cutting your fees just to get business in the door. Even worse is not doing anything, hoping that things will eventually either settle down or miraculously get better on their own.

What is the best thing to do in these situations? Before you make a decision that may do more harm than good, take a step back, take a deep breath, and give yourself some time to get out of desperation mode and into a more positive place. Once you do that, you can think more clearly and you can create more positive, long term, sustainable outcomes.

Here are some questions to ask yourself that will produce more value-based decisions.

1. **What is the breakdown I am addressing?** (By breakdown, I am not talking about a nervous breakdown but just all those annoying and totally inevitable interruptions that happen in our schedules every day.) What is the initial cause of your concern? Is it monetary issues or a weakened economy? Take time to identify what is causing the most headaches for you and your business or career.

2. **What is the desired outcome?** Is it simply dollars you want to deposit into your bank account? Or would you rather begin now to forge lasting relationships based on trust? The perfect time to create strong bonds between you, your clients, and your team, is during an economic slowdown. This gives you the time to concentrate on building solid relationships that will continue to grow once the economy shifts.

3. **How will it serve me, the company, or the business?** Making a hasty decision will always create havoc within your company. For example, before laying off members of your team, look at other unexplored avenues of generating income, or get creative in your advertising efforts. Carefully examine the long-term effects of any drastic decisions you make in order to simply save money. How will cost-cutting measures affect your levels of customer service? If you lose valuable people through layoffs, will you be able to hire them back at a later point?

4. **Is the decision in keeping with my values and the company's core values and visions?** When making decisions that will affect others, pay close attention to what your core values are telling

you. Gut instinct is seldom wrong. You know when you're going against everything you or your company stand for, because there will be a little voice telling you, "Hang on a second. This decision doesn't feel right." Listen carefully and act wisely.

5. **Will it produce long-term, sustainable results for the business?** What will be the impact of the decision you make today in one year, two years, or five years down the road? Will today's clients still be doing business with you in the future or will they have gone the route of the dinosaur and disappeared? Will implementing a change in the method of how you do business bring you continued client growth well into the days of tomorrow? Every action has long-term implications, so be sure to gauge potential future outcomes before you make your decision and act on it.

6. **Can you stand in your integrity if you make this decision?** This is the kicker. Can your heart and conscience live with the decisions your head has made? That's what decision making boils down to. If the decisions and actions you take affect your whole sense of well-being, something is off, and that means your integrity has been compromised. If you are unable to make a decision, implement the action, and stand by the results with quiet dignity, don't do it. Look for another solution to your problem.

After asking yourself these six questions, you should have a good idea of whether the decision you're about to make is a valid one that won't keep you up at night filled with dread about the outcome. And frankly, who wants to live the life of a terminal insomniac? I don't.

STEP THREE:
SETTING BOUNDARIES

"Boundaries are important.
Without them any old dog can come in your yard."

– Dr. Rachelle Disbennet Lee, PhD

The majority of the stress created in our lives is the result of not being able to set boundaries. By definition, the word boundary means to set a limit—a line not to be crossed. In all probability, you have allowed people to step over your boundaries for so long that you've forgotten where the boundary is.

Over time you have given away your integrity, your dignity, your self-esteem, and most of all, your power. And more than likely those dreaded "double R's", resentment and resignation, have set in and you feel powerless to change it. The "it" is your life and how you feel because you have allowed others to drive your life because you were afraid to speak up.

As much as we have grown and evolved, I still hear the same comments from my clients when they come to me for coaching. Things like, "I'm overwhelmed; I don't have enough time; I can't say no," and, "I feel guilty when I set boundaries." But breathe a sigh of relief because you *can* change yourself and your actions!

One of the problems with setting boundaries is this: it is not that we can't set them; it's that we don't give ourselves *permission* to set boundaries. If permission is an issue for you, try the next Action Exercise.

▶ *Action Exercise 7*
PERMISSION TO SET BOUNDARIES

"I, _____, give myself permission to set boundaries in my life so that I can

achieve more productivity, prosperity, and fulfillment, with less stress."

Matter of fact, you may want to take two or three index cards and write this sentence on them. Keep one on your desk, one at home, and one in your day planner. The bottom line is to keep this affirmation where you can see it, read it, and practice it daily.

The next boundary issue I would like to talk about is how consistent you are at setting your boundaries. A colleague and I were having a discussion about boundaries one day and she said something that really made me think. She said, "Setting boundaries is all fine and dandy, but what really matters is whether you set them in sand or stone. "Hmm, pretty interesting comment, isn't it?

My friend's comment reminded me of struggles with setting boundaries on the road to success in my own life. You've heard the saying, "When there is a lesson to be learned, a teacher appears." Believe me, I have had plenty of teachers! The reason for this is that every time you set a boundary, someone will appear who will test you, to see if you are serious or not. And I have found that the first ones to test you will be your own family. The most obvious ones will be your parents and your children. Why? *Emotional heartstrings*— you know, those sticky little strings that can tie you up in knots and cause huge pangs of guilt. And believe me, if you were raised as an Italian Catholic like I was, our mothers were so good at it that they could have been *travel agents for guilt trips.* Hence the reason it took me a lot longer to free myself from those sticky strings.

Boundaries that are set in sand eventually will wash away with the tide of change. These are what I call the "I'll try" boundaries. "I'll try" is what you say to those people who ask you to do something for them, but you are too emotionally attached to them to come right out and say, "No, I can't do that." So, we revert back to saying, "I'll try" to their request as we're scared that we might hurt their feelings or lose them as friends, spouses, lovers, or however they're tied to us emotionally, if we come straight out and say *no.*

My biggest teachers were, and still are, my family whom I love deeply. Thanks to them constantly testing my commitment, I have become a poster child for setting boundaries. As a result, I have become stronger and more committed to myself and my intentions because they are always willing to give me opportunities to practice saying no to some of their requests.

How many times do you catch yourself saying, "I'll try"?

Sitting on the "I'll try" fence opens up a whole can of worms for us because we are not living an authentic life. Not only are we not putting a value on our own personal feelings and time, we are totally disregarding the most important person in our life—ourselves! By being wishy-washy and not stating how we feel about that person's request, we say, "I'll try" which nine times out of 10 turns into a *yes*. Then we end up being ticked off at ourselves for not having enough backbone to have said no right from the get-go.

So, how (or perhaps more importantly, with whom) are you setting your "stone" boundaries? Can you honestly look at your Mom, child, or boss, and say, "No, that won't work for me"? Or can you say no to your husband or wife when he or she says, "Can you stop what you are doing right now to go take care of something for me?" Can you say no to a client who wants you to meet them after five o'clock or on a Saturday to finish up some business? Sure you can do it, but do you give yourself permission to do so? Ah, the sticky strings that really test your boundaries and can lead to sabotage.

Let's take a look at some of what I call *boundary saboteurs* that might show up in your life and how you can handle them.

Relationships that drain your energy

Do you have people in your life who suck the life right out of you? I bet you can feel your body tightening up already just thinking about them. Everything out of their mouth is negative and they suffer from the "poor me" syndrome. You tolerate these people because you just don't want to hurt their feelings by telling them the truth, but what about *your feelings* and *your boundaries*? You remember those, don't you?

If a relationship is bringing you down, then it may be time to do something about it. It doesn't mean that the person you're dealing with is a bad person; it just means that the two of you are in different places in your lives and the relationship is no longer working for you. In this scenario, you have two choices.

◆ You can choose to stay and be miserable or…

◆ You can choose to end it and spend more time in relationships that support and uplift you. I do hope you choose the latter.

This next Action Exercise will help you to sort this out.

▶ Action Exercise 8
"FRIENDS IN MY LIFE" LIST

Make a list of the friends you have in your life. Put a check mark by the ones that lift you up, and put an X by the ones that bring you down in words or deeds. Next take action to rid yourself of draining relationships. And if "negative Norah" persists in calling you up daily to tell you all about her latest drama du jour, then it may be time to intervene in the conversation. For example, calmly interrupt her by asking, "So, what do you *really* want Norah?" This question will make her stop and think about what she wants which in turn will help dispel some of her negativity. If she doesn't get off her pity pot, then it's time for you to reexamine your relationship with her to see if you want to be a willing participant in her ongoing melodrama.

Make a promise to yourself to surround yourself *only* with those friends that lift you up and support you.

Learning how to say "No" and mean it

This is a tall order for such a short word. It has been said that *no* is one of the most feared words in the English language. For me, I think it was especially hard to learn how to say no because of my ingrained Southern people-pleasing traits. I could think about the word, but to actually say no out loud was not even a choice I felt I had. I was taught that if my mother said, "The moon is made out of cream cheese," I was to reply, "Yes, ma'am" and off I went to get the crackers. What can I say? I was trained to serve and serve is what I did, well into my adult life.

You can't imagine what a shock it was to find out when I got older (much older, and much later in my life), that I actually had a choice to say no to someone. Prior to this newfound learning, I would say *yes* to almost all requests made to me whether I wanted to or not because I didn't want to hurt anyone else's feelings. *Never mind about my own feelings.* Come to think about it, I didn't know I was even allowed to have those feelings!

Learning this new skill did not come easy to me as I kept waiting for my Mom to jump out from behind the kitchen door and punish me. At first the word *no* sounded really harsh and definitely not becoming for a Southern gal like myself. I kept trying to sugar coat it and would use the words "maybe" or "I'll try" to make it sound less abrasive instead of coming right out and saying no.

When I first started practicing using this word, I would instead say, "I decline." Don't ask me why that sounded better to me, but it worked for me. One thing that I noticed when I started saying it was that people started taking me more seriously, and in turn I also started taking myself more seriously as well. As I became more comfortable with stepping out of my comfort zone, I then moved on to saying, "No, that won't work for me." To this day, this is still my favorite response. My second favorite saying is, "I have a previous commitment." End of story, no discussion.

What I learned was that it was not so much the actual word *no* itself, but the fear that came up by having to justify it after I said it out loud. Then I came to the realization that the more confident I became in myself and the more I trusted myself, the less I had to justify my decisions to others. I was finally saying *yes* to me. What a fabulous feeling! I promise you will feel this way too!

Here's an Action Exercise to help you flex those *no* muscles.

▶ Action Exercise 9
SAY YES TO ME

Write down in a notebook how many times you say no in a week and the date you did it. Start off stating no to the small requests and build up refusing to do the big ones. Celebrate yourself every time you do manage to say no and stick to it. You're going to love how good you feel about yourself.

Here's an affirmation I used to say when I first started flexing my no muscles and it really helped me feel more confident. **"Every time I say *NO* to someone else, I say *YES* to *ME*."**

The following is one of the biggest complaints I get from people who are practicing the fine art of saying no and sticking to it. "Someone is always coming in my office with questions. I can't get any work done!

There is a saying, "Your office is just an extension of your living room," and this is very true. If you have problems setting boundaries at home in your personal life, you will more than likely have problems setting boundaries at work. For example, let's say you're an executive or a manager who has an open door policy in your company. Because of this policy, you don't want to close the door to your office for fear that you might not appear to be open to listening to what members of your team have to say. As a result, you don't get any quiet time to do your work because people have a tendency to just barge in to talk with you.

Just because you have this policy in place does not mean you have to be the doormat at the entryway. Contrary to popular belief, you *do* have the option to close your door, ask to not be disturbed, and set boundaries and expectations around when you will be available for questions and conversations. You did not arrive at a leadership position by overextending your own boundaries, so why would you allow your employees to take advantage of you in this manner? Just imagine how much more productive you will be if you learn to set boundaries not only in your professional life but in your personal life too!.

Here's an example of a conversation you can use to establish a boundary respectfully. Say, "I'm busy right now, but I do want to talk to you about this issue. I have three o'clock available this afternoon. Would that work for you?"

You've clearly set a boundary stating when you're available and your coworkers or your employees will respect you for doing so. You will be able to better schedule your time with fewer interruptions, and ultimately be more productive and effective as a direct result of doing so. Plus you will have succeeded in role modeling what it means to be an effective leader.

Setting boundaries and taking back your power takes time, and you will need all the support you can get. Remembering these simple steps will help accelerate your efforts to create the success you want.

◆ Get clear about your intentions. What are you committed to doing in your business and in your life?

◆ Give yourself permission to say no.

◆ Ask yourself if this is something you really want to do or are you doing it out of guilt. Nine times out of ten your inner guilt critic will be talking to you. Take time to check in with yourself and remember where you were going in the first place.

◆ Starting off with small requests gives you more time to practice saying that word *no*.

- Practice, practice, practice! In the beginning, you may not be able to say no every time you want to. Forgive yourself, learn from the experience, and move on. Tomorrow is another day.

Keep in mind always, it doesn't matter where you start, *you just have to start.*

 *Lagniappe*

JUST SAY NO TO GUILT TRIPS

"Guilt is the gift that keeps on giving."

~ Erma Bombeck

I just cracked up laughing when I read this quote. It brought me back to a time in my life when my mother would send me on those *"Five Star Guilt Trips"* without ever booking a flight! I never packed my suitcase or left the couch, but there I was, off on another miserable one way, no refund, no fun, non-vacation to Guilt Trip Land! It was a vicious cycle. I would say no and then my Mom would make me feel so guilty that I would give in. It wasn't until I was much older that I learned how to deal with these guilt trips, set my boundaries in stone, and stand my ground.

I finally learned that in order to get past allowing others to put me on a guilt trip, I had to get clear about what and who was causing them. Here's what I discovered about being an unwilling traveler on the self-imposed guilt trips.

1. **You rent out space in your head to other people's behaviors and beliefs.** How many times have you sat around feeling guilty because of something someone has said to you? Their negative putdowns have taken up permanent residence in your brain causing you to freeze in your tracks, and mull over and over and over every single word they said until you believe it to be the truth. That's when guilt rears its ugly head and says, "I TOLD

you that if you didn't do... then there would be a price to pay. You DESERVE to feel miserable! Just look at what you did!" Blah! Blah! Blah!

Whenever this scenario happens, you have my permission to jump ship and choose another ocean liner because the vessel you're on, at some point, is going to sink faster than the Titanic! Listening to other's negative behaviors or accusations stirs up your inner critic—the part of you that doesn't believe you're a worthwhile human being. Stop letting people rent space in your head which causes you to feel guilty all the time! You deserve to have people in your life and business that totally support you and are positive, and only want the best for you. If they're not meeting those criteria, then you may have to take out the big electric eraser and remove them from your space.

2. **"You said you wanted to help out!"** I love this one! This is the response you get from people who can't understand why you actually had the nerve to say *no* to their request. They're not really big on setting boundaries and they can't fathom why you wouldn't want to give 10 hours a week of your already jampacked schedule to their wonderful cause, so their response to your no answer is to state, "Well, you said you wanted to help out. You're not going to make me go find someone else, are you?" This is when they start to twist the knife to make you really feel guilty. And if you're not clear about your intention, this will take you on a trip through the wilderness. Just remember, you decide what helping out looks like to you.

3. **"What do you mean... you don't want to listen to all my problems?"** The nerve of you! How dare you not want to fill up time in your day and precious real estate in your head with somebody else's problems? Some friends and employees just want to go on and on for the sake of talking to anyone who will listen. Don't get me wrong. There are times when you just have to vent for a few minutes, but then you need to move on

to finding a solution. However, last time I looked this was still America, land of the free, and you get to choose how you spend your time and who you want to listen to.

The bottom line is this: the reason that people try to guilt you is that somewhere along the way you gave permission for them to do this. Now it is time to take back that permission and set some boundaries around what's acceptable and what's not acceptable in your world. When you do this, it frees up a whole lot of real estate in your head to be more creative, more productive, and more successful in your life and your business.

It all starts with getting rid of old strategies that don't work in order to develop new proven strategies that will work.

STEP FOUR:
SAY WHAT YOU MEAN AND MEAN WHAT YOU SAY

"If you can't be direct, why be?"

– Lily Tomlin

When I read this quote, I immediately thought of all the amazing people I have had the honor to coach. Whether they were at the top of their game or just starting their climb up the ladder of success, there is one universal challenge that they all struggled with and wanted to improve—negotiating and handling difficult conversations. Whenever we are working on this often trying area of change, I'm constantly telling them, "Quit beating around the bush trying to be nice. If you want to be heard, you have to say what you mean and mean what you say." Beating around the bush and never coming straight out and asking for what you want only serves one purpose—it flushes out any stray animals that might be lurking in that certain piece of shrubbery!

Many people, women in particular, have been trained in the art of sugarcoating and what I like to call verbal dancing. We dance around the subject we most want to discuss, thinking that the other person will get what we are alluding to and eventually we will get what we want. Not! The only thing you get from a conversation like that is frustration. It doesn't matter that the other person might be a friend, partner, business associate, or boss; we still camouflage our words with honey so they can slide into the ears of the listener more easily. Heaven forbid that we rock the status quo by actually saying what we *really* want to say! After all, how would we survive if that other person did not like us after they find out what we *really* thought? Here's a better question for you. How's that sugarcoating been working for you?

Every time you sugarcoat or dance around an issue, you

diminish your capacity and self-worth. You give away your power, your integrity, and your dignity. And most of all, you wind up being frustrated, resentful, and resigned because you're not getting what you want. You can be yourself. Be the unique person that you are, be direct, and be taken seriously when you say what you mean and mean what you say.

It is up to us to make the choice to quit putting a spin on our words out of fear of repercussion, to that of respectfully, calmly, and clearly stating our wants and desires without fear of rejection from others. I know it can be done. I learned how to be direct and say what I mean, and so can you.

I want you to ask yourself these two direct questions.

◆ What is the price I pay for sugarcoating my conversations?

◆ Is this how I really want to spend the rest of my life?

Standing in your integrity and speaking what's right for you may not always be the easiest road to travel, but it is going to be the one that brings the most rewards for you. With that being said, let's move on to why you don't get what you want.

Do you ever wonder why you don't get what you want?

I suspect you were never taught that it was okay to ask for what you wanted, much less expect to get it. If you were a Southern, Italian, polite little Catholic girl like me, you were raised not to ask, but to wait for someone to offer things to you. And if they didn't offer, you kept quiet. Almost like the old saying that, "Children should be seen, but not heard."

Why do you think we women get the reputation of being whiny and manipulative? Because the only way we learned to ask for what we wanted was to gripe and nag until our parents or husbands eventually gave in and said yes! Or later in our adult life we would make statements like, "It really would be nice if I had more time to myself" or, "It would be great if I could get off early today." As a result of those same habits we learned as children, we suffered a whole lot of resentment and resignation because we didn't get what we wanted. Like I said, we were taught to be good little girls, not the high-powered women that we are today.

However, that was then—this is now. You can change this behavior trait by learning how to ask for what you want. Now that we're all grown up, we need to know how to ask for (and receive!) what we want with confidence, respect, and integrity, instead of nagging, whining, or complaining.

Learning how to make effective requests

Believe it or not, your power and your identity are directly tied to your ability to make effective requests. The test of a successful request is that it has a successful outcome and you can learn how to achieve this by incorporating the following four request components.

◆ A speaker

◆ A listener

◆ An action to be performed

◆ A time frame to be completed

Whether you're a top level executive in a huge corporation, an entrepreneur, a leader in a volunteer organization, or a stay-at-home parent, learning how to make effective requests is what's going to help you get you where you want to go. Let me give you an example of how this might show up for you. Here are some *ineffective* requests. See if you can relate to any of these.

◆ I need this report to go out.

◆ I need some help on this project.

◆ I wish I had more time off.

◆ I wish my team would do more.

It is no wonder we don't get what we want. When you make vague requests like the examples above, you get vague results. Then to top it off, you get mad when you don't get what you want. Imagine that. You get the results you want when you get specific in how you present your requests.

For example, here is a *much more effective request.*

"Sue, this report needs to be in the mail by 5:00 p.m. today. What obstacles do we need to overcome to ensure that this happens?"

Are you beginning to see the difference? The second request is very clear and concise. Sue didn't have to guess what the expectations were because her boss included all the details. This, in turn, makes it easy for Sue to respond to this call for action as nothing is left out of the instructions that were effectively communicated to her.

Does this mean you will always get what you want? No, it does not, but you will increase your effectiveness and outcome by using the above components when making requests.

I want to make a distinction here before we go any further. In order for a request to be a request, there has to be permission granted to the other person to decline. In other words, you need to be prepared to hear them say *no.* If their permission is not allowed, your request turns into a demand. Keep in mind there are instances where the guidelines or expectations of your position may not allow for the other person to say *no.* If that is the case, your request of them would be simply considered part of their job duties.

Here's where learning the skill of making powerful counter offers could come in to play. For example, the conversation could go like this.

"Mr. Smith, we will not be able to complete the report until tomorrow morning. I will be happy to call the recipient and let them know that we will be delivering it first thing in the morning."

The hardest part of learning how to make effective requests

is building up the courage and confidence to ask for what you want, hence the reason we dance around the issue instead of just asking. However, it does get easier every time you do it and you will feel more empowered every time you succeed in clearly stating what you want done. I know what you are probably saying to yourself right now, "Yeah, that's easy for you to say, Cookie, but..." No buts! This step was not easy for me to learn either, but the more I practiced, the better I got at doing it. My mouth finally quit quivering when I opened it to speak, and, as a matter of fact, I've gotten quite good at it, and so can you, with time.

I do know that when you are just starting out on the journey of learning how to make effective requests, you are going to be somewhat nervous, so I've included the next Action Exercise that will help you calm your nerves, get you grounded, and ready to take action.

▶ Action Exercise 10
HOW TO MAKE AN EFFECTIVE REQUEST

Here are the components involved in making effective requests.

◆ A speaker
◆ A listener
◆ An action to be performed
◆ A time frame to be completed

Using this component guide, ask yourself these questions.

◆ Who is the person I want to make the request to?
◆ What is my request?
◆ What do I want from them?
◆ What is my time frame to complete it?

Now, if need be, practice asking for what you need out loud in front of a mirror or with a friend with whom you feel comfortable. Most importantly, if you are not used to making requests, start off asking for small things. The more confidence you build in yourself in the beginning, the bigger the requests you can make down the road.

Since the hardest part of asking for what you want is getting up the courage to do so, this brings me to the next important step.

Meaning what you say

When you talk about saying what you mean and meaning what you say, you first have to address what has kept you from speaking up for yourself for so long.

It's like the proverbial white elephant in the room. Nobody talks about it, but it is always there, especially for women. That white elephant would be your fear. You know what I'm referring to—that feeling that has you quaking in your boots or that has your stomach churning when you're not sure of yourself or are in unfamiliar territory.

As I mentioned earlier, when I was growing up, there was not a whole lot of free speech going on in my house. If they said it was Easter, we dyed eggs. It was that simple.

One of my Mom's favorite sayings, especially if I did or said something that was totally unacceptable to her was, "What would the people think?" Yes, in those days, people-pleasing and looking good were twin sisters and they were alive and doing well in our world. As a result, it took me many years to learn how to just be who I was and say what I felt, with dignity, respect, and integrity for myself and others. I came to realize that I had to find my own voice and my own path. I had to address the fears that held me back or I would always be biting my tongue, second guessing myself, and giving away my personal power, and that, folks, was unacceptable to me.

The only way to address the fears and old beliefs that keep you stuck in one place is to identify them one by one. Make a determination as to whether they're real or imagined. I have a terrific Action Exercise that addresses this specific issue and will help you move forward.

▶ *Action Exercise 11*

WHAT ARE THE FEARS HOLDING YOU BACK?

List all the fears or old beliefs that keep you stuck. Here are some examples.

◆ What would the people think?

◆ They won't like me.

◆ They will leave me.

◆ I'm not enough.

◆ I might hurt their feelings.

◆ I'm not smart enough.

Now *you* finish this list with *your own* fears and old beliefs. Just add as many as you can think of, right now. As you think of more items, add them to the list. Remember, this is just a start. The point is to get them on paper where you can determine if they're real or imagined. You may be surprised to notice that many of the fears we carry around are just our interpretation of stories that we have told ourselves. Now it is time to let go of them and create a new story—one that empowers you. For example, start believing instead:

◆ I am enough!

◆ I am smart enough!

◆ I am worthy!

◆ I am confident!

◆ I do deserve to live a fulfilled, successful life!

One of my all time favorite books I read when I first started on my transformation journey was Susan Jeffers' book, *Feel the Fear and Do It Anyway*® (www.SusanJeffers.com). One of her teachings helped me make fear my friend as opposed to my enemy. These are the *Five Truths about Fear* from Susan's book—used with her permission—that support me when my own fears come up.

1. The fear will never go away as long as I continue to grow.

2. The only way to get rid of the fear of doing something is to go out... and do it.

3. The only way to feel better about myself is to go out... and do it.

4. Not only am I going to experience fear whenever I'm out on unfamiliar territory, but so is everyone else.

5. Pushing through fear is less frightening than living with the underlying fear that comes from a feeling of helplessness.

Sometimes we don't say what we mean for fear of hurting someone else's feelings

We dance around it and kind of, sort of, say something. This is people-pleasing at its finest. Every time you do this you give away your power, your dignity, and your self-respect, not to mention your integrity. We are so scared that we'll say the wrong thing at the wrong time that we literally say nothing at all. We either say nothing or blurt out one of those little half lies. You know what I mean... saying things like, "That color isn't the right shade of red for you" instead of saying, "That dress really does nothing to enhance your figure."

Learning skills that help you become an effective communicator is key to your success as a leader. You will create blame-free environments and relationships that foster integrity, cohesiveness, commitment, and motivation for all to thrive and succeed.

Whine you lose—Ask you receive

"Speaking your feelings is definitely a good thing,
but if you really want to make an impact,
you have to ask for what you want."

– Cookie Tuminello

There are those of us who live and speak totally from their feelings, and then there are those of us who have a hard time accessing those feelings because we are so bottom-line focused. Guess which one I was before I started doing this work? It wasn't that I didn't have feelings; it's just that I had a hard time expressing them. I would skip over the feelings part and go straight to what was working and what was not working for me. I can still do that, but now I can access my feelings to connect my head with my heart.

Speaking your feelings is definitely a good thing, but if you really want to make an impact, you have to ask for what you want. What do I mean by that? When we choose to speak up, it is usually because something is not working for us; someone did or said something that upset us or made us feel "less than." So, consequently we chose to tell them how we feel, and not always in a good way.

Just speaking your feelings is like blowing in the wind—it's not going to get you anywhere. And to top it off, it can come across as whining. Like I said earlier, this is why women get the bad rap of being whiners. This is a practice that diminishes your power and your dignity and it's time to do something different that works. So, how do you reclaim your power and dignity in this situation?

First of all, get clear about what it was that upset you in the first place before you speak your feelings. Do you need to get clarity about what they said? Did they say something that upset you and made you feel "less than"?

Second, decide what is it you want from the other person before you have the conversation. If you don't get clear about what it is that you want, then you are liable to sabotage yourself.

Third, clearly make the request for what you want.

Fourth, always remember that whenever you make a request, there must be permission for the other person to say *no*. This is a big deal because most people think that just because you ask someone for something they have to say *yes*. *Not so!*

Let me give you an example from my own experience. Many years ago I was working out at a local health club and the personal trainer had a nasty habit of putting people down and intimidating them. I was one of those people. One morning he made a comment that came across as a put down and I had had enough. This is how I responded.

"You do not have permission to speak to me that way. Your comments are hurtful and demeaning to me, and I request that you not ever do it again."

From that moment on, I was treated with respect and dignity. Oh, and in case you're wondering what the response was from the trainer… it was silence.

Take time to look at whether or not your conversations are producing the results you want. And if not, maybe it's time to speak up and get the support you need to have more powerful, positive conversations.

IS YOUR SILENCE COSTING YOU YOUR LIFE?

"When we speak, we are afraid our words
will not be heard or welcomed. But when we are silent,
we are still afraid. So it is better to speak."

– Audre Lorde

A major source of stress is caused by unspoken feelings, not getting what we want, and not asking for what we want. This stress can cause headaches, insomnia, emotional eating, avoidance, depression, and laryngitis, to name a few. I, myself, have experienced all of these telltale signs at one time or another in my life.

So, back to the question, is your silence causing you stress? A good question to ask yourself is whether your life is working or not working for you, and a good place to start looking into this aspect is to examine your relationship with yourself and others. Ask yourself the following questions to gain insight into this area.

◆ How many times do you say yes when you want to say no, for fear that that people may not like you? You valued the other person more than you valued yourself.

◆ How many times have you kept quiet because you were afraid to speak up, for fear of what might happen or you weren't sure of yourself? So, you just sucked it up and paid for it on the inside.

◆ How many times have you spoke your feelings, but did not ask for what you wanted, for fear that you didn't know how to ask or felt you weren't worthy enough? So, instead you kept silent and came away unfulfilled.

◆ How many times have you let others dictate the course of your life because you didn't think you knew enough? Instead you lived the life they wanted, not the life you wanted.

◆ How many times have you settled for less when you could have had more? What did that do to your self-worth?

Think about it. When you become silent, don't express your feelings, and don't speak up, you give away your power and your soul. Now, if this only happened once it may not be a problem; you learn from the experience and you take better care of yourself next time. However, keeping silent time after time causes a slow demise of the quality of your life, not to mention damaging your integrity, dignity, joy, passion, and prosperity. How long are you going to keep saying "Ouch!"?

So, how do you reclaim your power?

The first step is to be accountable. You are where you are because of the choices you have made in your life. Now don't go south on me and start beating yourself up more. It's not bad or wrong—it's just where you were at the time. Now it is time to make better choices. Stand up for yourself!

The second step is taking a look at the areas of your life where you've sabotaged yourself. Determine what it is that you want and start putting in corrections. In other words, you start taking different actions than the ones you took before. And every time you take a new empowered action, you begin to reclaim your power little by little. *Remember the saying, "How do you eat an elephant? One bite at a time."* That adage definitely applies here to breaking your silence and speaking up for yourself.

STEP FIVE:
MASTERING THE ART
OF PRESENTING IDEAS
AND HANDLING
DIFFICULT CONVERSATIONS

"Your own words are the bricks and mortar
of the dreams you want to realize.
Your words are the greatest power you have.
The words you choose and their use establish
the life you experience."

– Sonia Choquette

One of the challenges I hear from professionals most frequently is, "My boss won't listen to my ideas. I see lots of opportunities to make the company more successful, but every time I approach him/ her, I get immediately shot down. How do I get my boss to really listen and to accept my proposals?"

First of all, you can't force your boss to do anything, but you can set the stage for the best possible outcome if you create a plan of action before you meet.

The two main reasons people have trouble communicating powerful ideas is: **1)** their own lack of self-confidence, and **2)** they don't get clear about what they want before they have the conversation and end up coming across as not being fully prepared.

Your ability to be an effective communicator is the building block to realizing your dreams. Your power and your identity is defined by your ability to make powerful requests, present powerful ideas, and handle difficult conversations with ease. Consequently, the degree to which you are competent at getting your point across clearly and succinctly is the degree to which you are successful in both your professional and personal life.

There are two types of conversations that I have observed. One is what I laughingly refer to as *cocktail talk* which is mostly idle chitchat spoken just to pass time and fill up space. Then there is another form of conversation that I call *conscious speaking*. Let me give you one of my favorite examples of each. The conversations go like this.

Cocktail Talk—A friend says, "Let's get together for lunch soon." You reply, "That sounds great. I would love to do that." You both say goodbye, go your merry way, and before you get to your car you've forgotten what the question was. Can you relate?

Conscious Speaking—A friend says, "Let's get together for lunch soon." You reply, "That sounds great. What day is good for you next week?" This conversation is more conscious and deliberate than the first example.

If I am going to be up to creating big things in my life, do you honestly think I'm going to just let my words hang out in the universe without any direction? Do you think that I am going to wait for someone else to determine my destiny? I don't think so. I bet you can guess which type of conversation I engage in most of the time. Life is too short to waste it on all that empty talk.

That's not to say you can't chitchat or enjoy casual conversations. There is a time and place for both types of connecting. However, when it comes to your business, your career, your livelihood, and your important relationships, you will want to be more conscious and deliberate in your communication skills.

Clear, concise, conscious communication is the key to your ultimate success. When you master this important function, you increase your potential for favorable results and you manage conflicts more successfully.

In order to help you create more positive results, the communication guidelines that I've created will help you get to where you want to go faster while eliminating sugarcoating and verbal dancing.

Being able to communicate professionally and comfortably is what my clients strive for. Here are the three components that will help you do this more effectively.

How well you know yourself

You must first learn to trust yourself so that in turn you can trust others by building up your own level of self-confidence. The more comfortable you become in your own skin, the easier you are able to communicate comfortably and professionally with others.

How well you handle breakdowns

By breakdowns, I am not talking about a full-blown nervous breakdown, but just all those annoying and totally inevitable interruptions that happen in our schedules every day. There will always be breakdowns in your life—they're not the problem. The problem is when you allow them to stop your flow of action and put you in a bad mood for the rest of the day. This in turn tears down your productivity, your power, and ultimately your profit. What can I say? Stuff happens all the time, but the bottom line is this: When breakdowns happen in your life, handle them, learn from them, and move on.

How well you communicate

You can have the greatest ideas in the world, but if you can't communicate those ideas effectively, you are dead in the water.

The two reasons that you get blindsided in conversations and don't get what you want is because: **1)** you don't get clear about what you want before you have the conversation, and **2)** your lack of confidence.

Self-confidence

"Self-confidence is a special elixir that Spirit has prepared to help each of us face and surmount the challenges of life. It's an aromatic blending of invigorating essences,

attitude, experience, wisdom, optimism, and faith."

– Sarah Ban Breathnach

When I ask my clients what they'd like more of in their life, the most common response is more self-confidence. Immediately I think back to when I used to feel like that. For some reason we think it's a gene we didn't get at birth. Well, I've got a news flash for you. We've *all* got that gene! We just haven't always known how to use it effectively, hence the reason we settle for less than what we want and deserve in our lives, and ultimately never reach the top of the success ladder. Here's what I've learned about self-confidence that has helped me become more patient and accepting of myself.

◆ Self-confidence comes from competence.

◆ Competence comes from practice.

◆ Practice comes from knowledge.

◆ Knowledge comes from learning (education).

A couple of years ago I was knee deep in the process of making changes to my business branding, website, programs, and services. This whole experience felt like I was emerging out of the Dark Ages and being slammed headfirst into the 21st century. It required me to educate myself about website presence, Internet marketing, and copywriting. I studied feverishly and worked with competent professionals who taught me the new skills I needed to know to get me where I wanted to go. As a result of this immersion process, I became more confident. Now I don't freeze up as much when someone says "html" or "back end automation." That education helped me become confident enough to create my step-by-step system and share it in this book with you.

So, how do you become an effective communicator? **You plan, you orchestrate, you implement!**

Whether you are a high-powered executive, a mid-level

manager, an employee asking for a raise, or a spouse discussing a large purchase with your partner, you struggle with the same issues. The following guidelines will help you communicate in a way that begets the respect and dignity you deserve. Does this mean you will always get what you want? No, it does not, but it does mean that you will feel more empowered and be taken more seriously when you speak. Lee Iacocca said it very succinctly, "You can have brilliant ideas, but if you can't get them across, your ideas won't get you anywhere."

This next Action Exercise will help you plan, orchestrate, and implement. Keep in mind that this exercise can be used when presenting ideas to management, peers, family, or friends.

▶ *Action Exercise 12*

GUIDELINES FOR PRESENTING IDEAS AND SOLUTIONS EFFECTIVELY

First and foremost, before you start designing your conversation, request a scheduled time or an appointment with the person to whom you'd like to speak. Don't wait for an opportunity to present itself, such as catching them in the hallway or waiting for them to be in a good mood. *Successful people create their own opportunities.*

Remember, the key is to be solution-oriented, not problem-focused. Use the following guidelines to design your conversation before you open your mouth to speak.

◆ What is your intention/purpose for having this conversation?

◆ What is the breakdown you are addressing? What's working? What's not working?

◆ What is your proposed idea?

◆ How will it benefit the company/department/self or employer?

◆ How will your proposed plan work?

◆ Who and what will it require?

- How long will it take? Use specific time frames.

- Do you anticipate any breakdowns? How will you address them?

- What is the cost of the project, if any?

- What is your commitment to participation in the plan?

- What support will you need from management/others?

- After completing a presentation, always ask for questions, feedback, and commitments to a proposed plan so that everyone is clear about their roles.

Use these solution-oriented guidelines as you practice getting your thoughts together. If you need to role play with someone, choose someone you know and trust. Role playing helps build your self-confidence and gets you grounded. I do this exercise with my clients all the time and it really works.

A few years ago, when I first moved to Lafayette, I had the honor of being featured as the cover story for a regional magazine. I was so impressed with the professionalism of the magazine, the layout, articles, and the editor that I wanted to be a part of their team and write a regular column for them. So, I did some research on the magazine and then called the editor and set a time for us to get together for coffee. Being the social Southerners that we are, we like to do most everything over coffee or lunch. Before meeting with her, I created a list of questions and answers that I wanted to cover in my initial talk to get clear on how the process was going to go. Here are some questions I asked myself before our meeting:

- Q: What is my intention or purpose for having this conversation?
  A: My intention in having this conversation is to propose adding a life-skills column to their magazine. I want to contribute and add value for the readers and the magazine.

- Q: What is the breakdown I am addressing?
  A: There was no breakdown per se in this incident, just a niche

that was not being addressed. The magazine is geared toward providing information, articles, etc., to support women in living healthy, happy, informed, fulfilled lives. During my research, I noticed that there were no articles that dealt specifically with women as a whole, such as life skills to live happier, more authentic lives personally and professionally.

◆ **Q:** What is my proposed idea?
A: My idea is to offer to provide monthly articles that speak to this subject matter.

◆ **Q:** How will it benefit the company, department, myself or the employer?
A: The way that it will benefit readers of the magazine is to add another dimension and good content to an already successful magazine.

◆ **Q:** How will my proposed plan work?
A: I will provide them with three sample columns for editor and publisher perusal. Provided they are pleased with the content, we can discuss details of a co-venture. This is a win-win relationship for both parties.

◆ **Q:** Who and what will be required to make it happen?
A: Provided we have an agreement, all that I will require are deadline due dates and any topics of interest. We can go from there.

◆ **Q:** How long will it take? What are my specific time frames?
A: I will submit sample articles to them by tomorrow for their perusal and we can set up a time to do a follow-up call on Friday, if that would work for them.

◆ **Q:** Do I anticipate any breakdowns?
A: I don't foresee any breakdowns.

◆ **Q:** What is the cost of the project, if any?
A: No cost to either party.

◆ **Q:** What will be my commitment to the plan?
A: I am making a commitment to deliver articles to the magazine in accordance with the deadline dates.

As you can see by these detailed questions, I prepared for the interview by anticipating and reviewing all the questions and answers I thought I might encounter. I felt confident that at the end of that meeting, the editor would have all the information she needed to make an informed decision on whether or not to proceed.

Knowing when to speak and when not to speak

> *"Speak when you are angry and you will make the best speech you will ever regret."*
>
> *– Ambrose Bierce*

I think we can all relate to this quote. The regret comes when you realize what you've done and you wish you could cut your tongue out, or hit the "delete" button and take it all back. If you speak when you're angry, you are only reacting to being attacked or expressing the need to be right. In either case, nothing gets resolved. The old adage *"You can be right or you can be happy"* still holds true. If you want to be happy and successful, you have to talk to, not at, the other person, and you have to listen to the other person's concerns. You're probably thinking right now that you would just as soon knock them in the head with a two-by-four. I can relate to that! However, I would recommend that you take a few deep breaths, go off to a neutral corner, and think before you speak. Communication is about win-win, not win-lose scenarios. It's about building relationships, not tearing them down.

Before we go into the guidelines for handling difficult conversations, let's talk about what happens when conflict arises.

According to Webster's *New World Dictionary,* the definition of conflict is to be antagonistic, fight, war, sharp disagreement, emotional disturbance.

No wonder we have trouble dealing with conflict! Just the mere word has such negative connotations. Personally, I prefer to use the phrase *difficult conversations* instead of the word *conflict*.

What happens to you when you have to respond to conflict? What is the first thing that pops into your head? The fight or flight reaction, correct? All of our fears of rejection and past experiences start flashing before our very eyes. Where does that come from? It comes from not knowing yourself, not trusting yourself, and what you learned and from what you experienced as a child.

Here's what I know for sure: You can choose to be a victim of your fears or you can choose to be empowered by them. The choice is yours.

What's the solution?

You remember I said that self-confidence comes from competence? Well, here is where you educate yourself by learning skills that will help you handle those difficult conversations with more confidence and ease. And you won't get blindsided nearly as much.

Now, does this mean you will always get what you want? Once again, no, it does not, but it does mean you create a more positive environment for the best possible outcome. And you will feel more empowered and be taken more seriously when you speak.

Action Exercise 13 is going to help you build communication skills and feel more confident and courageous about having difficult conversations. Don't skip it!

▶ *Action Exercise 13*

GUIDELINES FOR HANDLING DIFFICULT CONVERSATIONS

Preparation—What kind of conversation do you want to have? Some examples might be: clarity, completion, handle breakdowns, take action, closure, etc.

Intention/Purpose—What do you want to happen in this conversation? What is the intended outcome? Set the context at the beginning for where you want to go.

What is the breakdown you are addressing?—What is working or not working?

What do you need from this person? What is your request? Be specific.

When do you need it? Be clear about your expectations.

Ask for questions, feedback, and elicit commitment from all parties involved.

Here's a great example of a conversation between a manager and an employee about the employee's habit of being late for work.

Manager: "Sue, I would like to have a conversation regarding your tardiness this past month. It has been reported to me that you have been late daily for two weeks in a row, and that your tardiness has created a lack of productivity and effectiveness in daily duties. In addition, it is not setting a good example for the other employees who do get to work on time every day. The expectations and guidelines were made clear in the initial hiring interview. Clearly something is not working. What is it going to take for you to get back on track? How can I support you? I will do my part. However, here's what I want you to know. If you are late one more time, there will be consequences for your actions which will result in dismissal. That being said, do you have any questions or comments at this time? If not, are you willing to honor your commitment to get to work on time?"

This scenario covers just the manager's response to the problem so that you have an idea of how to move through this type of difficult conversation more professionally and comfortably. There will always be excuses as to why the employee did or did not do what they had promised. The important thing is to not get caught up in the excuses but to stay focused on what's working and not working and what action you want them to take now.

Once you begin to practice and use the guidelines, here are some added communication tips that will support you in having more successful conversations.

◆ Always be solution oriented, not problem focused.

◆ Always treat the action that's being or not being performed, not the person.

◆ Never start a sentence with *you did*.

◆ Never play the blame game. Be accountable for your actions.

◆ Never whine and complain unless you plan on taking action.

◆ Never whine to someone other than the person you have the complaint with. *It tears down your integrity.*

◆ Always replace phrases like, "It won't work," with, "How can we make this work?"

◆ Always start your sentences with, "I choose to do this," instead of, "I need to do this."

I know that this sounds like a lot to take in, but I can promise that if you plan, orchestrate, and implement these communication skills, you will feel more confident. And the biggest perk of all is that you will feel more like the empowered, successful person you were born to be.

CREATING BLAME-FREE ENVIRONMENTS

"When you throw dirt, you lose ground."

~ *Texas Proverb*

Nothing tears down relationships, teamwork, effectiveness, and productivity like the office rumor mill and gossip. Some refer to this as water-cooler chitchat. There are some individuals who will go straight to the source to handle a breakdown. There are others who will complain and whine to everyone but the person with whom they have a grievance.

The problem is not that these breakdowns occur; the problem is that they don't get handled when they come up. This ultimately causes a disconnect in relationships because there is a big white elephant in the room that nobody wants to talk about, causing everyone to tiptoe around it, trying to avoid the minefield. This behavior tears down trust, integrity, confidence, productivity, and positive communication.

What can you do to abate these breakdowns and create what I call a blame-free environment in which everyone thrives and succeeds?

First of all, let me explain what a blame-free environment means. The name says it all. It means truly blame-free. The environment is solution focused, not problem focused. It means there are no victims, only victories. The focus is on the mission and intentions of the group, not on being right. It's about building trust, confidence, and open communication within the group so that people are able to handle these breakdowns when they come up and move beyond them.

How do you create this blame-free environment? It starts at the top with the leader of the group. Let's face it. You have to role model what it is that you want to create among your team if you want them to emulate your behavior.

I believe that by giving your team the necessary tools to handle these breakdowns, you can create a blame-free environment that begets feedback, openness, trust, and skills to handle these breakdowns when they occur and in some cases prevent them from happening altogether.

Here are three steps to creating a blame-free environment:

1. Integrity has to start at the top of the food chain. One of the best definitions I found of this powerful word is "integrity is consistency of actions, values, methods, measures, principles, expectations, and outcomes." Great leadership is a skill that is often shown more than taught. The example you set is key to getting others to follow your lead. Don't expect your team members to stick to hour-long lunches if you, as their boss, routinely take two-hour escapes from the office.

2. Building Trust. The whole team supports each other and is committed to one goal—the success of their mission. You tell the truth, come from a place of integrity, and do what you say you are going to do. And if you can't honor your commitment, you acknowledge it to the other party, or you have a conversation to clean it up so that you can move on. It's about creating win-win relationships.

3. Communication. Learn how to handle breakdowns when they come up and don't let them hang on for too long. Remember the saying, *"One bad apple can ruin a whole bushel."* Well, that holds true for teams. You must always keep in mind that the intention is always to be solution oriented. It's not about who did it but what is best for the team and overall goals of the group. You can be right or you can be happy and successful. The choice is yours.

By incorporating integrity, trust, and solid communication skills into your company's overall performance, the sky is the limit to achieving success in your goals. And with today's uncertain economy, who doesn't want to be on a winning team?

STEP SIX:
PLAN TO SUCCEED DAILY

"Wake up Alice, this ain't Wonderland.
Wishing and hoping for things to change in your life
is not going to cut it.
The Good-Change Fairy is not going to come
and sprinkle pixie dust on you and make everything
in your life all better. Things in your life don't change
until you take action to change them.
Life is about change, and change is about taking a chance on
something or someone like you.
The quality of your life depends on it."

– Cookie Tuminello

Nothing changes in your life until you take some action. Not just any old action, but conscious action. All of the steps and Action Exercises in the previous chapters will mean nothing unless you set the stage and create the environment for success to take place. What do I mean by this? It's obvious that you can't keep doing the same things you've been doing and expect different results, as that's the definition of insanity. Change is not going to just mysteriously happen in your life. You need to make a conscious decision that you want to change, then set the wheels in motion and get moving.

Does this scenario sound familiar? You start your day off in a dead heat run and before you get to the office you're already fried. Then once there, you're met with one breakdown after another, and the day goes downhill from that moment on. If this is you, how's that working for you? I'm guessing it's not working too well or you wouldn't be reading this book. I'm starting to get hyper just thinking about it because I used to be just like that. Before you say, "Yeah, but Cookie..." just stop, take a breath, and hear me out.

You must first plan to be successful in order to be successful. For example, you don't dress for the job you have, you dress for the job you want. I know. Sounds kind of hokey doesn't it, but truer words were never spoken. Here are some strategies that will help you set the stage to succeed daily, right from the first day of a new year.

Ease into your day

Get up 20 minutes earlier than you normally would just to have a quiet cup of coffee and do some automatic writing. Automatic writing means that your thoughts flow from your pen without any critic sitting on your shoulder and without any regard for punctuation, grammar, or "making sense." In other words, it is a brain dump.

Automatic writing (Julia Cameron calls this practice "doing morning pages") clears your head, which is on race mode when you wake up, and boosts your creativity. And who can't use more creativity? You can use any handy, spiral notebook for your morning pages because no one is going to see your words but you—unless you choose to share them.

To find out more about this practice and how it can boost your creativity, check out Julia Cameron's book, *"The Artist's Way"*.

Start every day with a motivational quote or reading

I always incorporate this part into my morning ritual. I purchase a new daily inspirational book every year, and each day it always seems to speak to whatever is going on in my life. Here are some daily inspiration books by some of my favorite authors to help you get started: Melody Beattie's *Journey to the Heart;* Sue Patton Thoele's *The Woman's Book of Soul*; Eileen Caddy's *Opening Doors Within;* and Iyanla Vanzant's *Faith in the Valley*.

▶ *Action Exercise 14*

EACH MORNING, WRITE AN INTENTION STATEMENT FOR THE DAY

A *daily intention statement* is not a to-do list; it is statement about what you want your day to look like—the context of your day. You could say that it is the container for your actions and focus for the day. Here's an example of the one that I frequently use.

"Today my intention is to only think about, talk about, bring about, and be about that which I want to create in my life", i.e., focus, creativity, connection, completion of project, client attraction, business development, writing, etc.

I bet you're thinking right now, "You want me to do all of these steps first thing in the morning? Are you kidding me?" No, I'm not. All of these take me about 30 minutes to do and two leisurely, heavenly cups of coffee. And believe me, there are some days I wish I could make this *me time* last all day. Think about it! Aren't you worth 30 minutes of quiet, alone time in the morning?

Get rid of the clutter in your life—from closet to office

Clutter equates to procrastination and hampers your creativity. Put unused items back into use by recycling, having a garage sale, or contributing to a charity that resells them. For instance, if you've got clothes in your closets that you haven't looked at, let alone worn, in the last two years, get rid of them. If you've got magazine articles or materials that have been stacked on your desk for months, get rid of those, too. Chances are if you haven't read them yet, you're not going to. Besides, nowadays you will most likely find that 90% of those articles you've been meaning to read are posted on the Internet. How will you ever bring new things into your life if there is no room for them, physically or spiritually?

Choose to see mistakes as learning opportunities

Do you remember when you were learning how to ride a bike? You got on the bike and then probably fell off a bunch of times before you got the hang of it, but pretty soon, with practice, you didn't fall off anymore. The same principle for riding a bike is true for achieving the success you want in your life. I can tell you that I have fallen off my bike many, many times. I get up, I learn, I grow, and I go. It may take me a little longer, but I'm getting there. I have no intention of letting mistakes or missteps get in my way.

Multiply the good things when you express gratitude

If you want to experience more abundance in your life, write down three things each morning for which you're grateful. Make the first item on your list, "I am grateful for me." Acknowledge yourself first; it's easy to forget that's where it all starts. By taking the time to notice and put these things in writing, you will begin to recognize and receive more good outcomes. Gratitude has a funny way of multiplying the good things that come to us each day. Being grateful doesn't hurt a soul *and it ends up feeding yours.*

▶ Action Exercise 15
WHAT AM I GRATEFUL FOR TODAY?

By putting this step into practice, you will start to recognize and receive more good things in your life. Do this Action Exercise, in conjunction with morning pages, for 30 days and see what kind of impact it has on your life.

1. Today I am grateful for _____
_____.

2. Today I am grateful for _____
_____.

3. Today I am grateful for _____
_____.

Focus on the present. The future will take care of itself.

If you spend your today worrying about what tomorrow will bring, you've missed out on 24 hours of living... period. Why do you think they call it the "present?" Simply because it is a gift, so treat it with care and enjoy every minute of every hour in the day. This day will not happen again.

At the end of the day, make a list of all the tasks you completed instead of focusing on the one task you did not complete.

You will find that this is much more productive than looking at the list of things you haven't finished. Not only will you feel good about having completed some of those to-do items, you'll have even fewer of them to look at tomorrow morning.

▶ Action Exercise 16
WHAT I ACCOMPLISHED TODAY

Write down the top 10 things you completed today.

The intention behind having my clients complete this Action Exercise is that, at the end of the day, most of us have an uncanny knack for only focusing on the one thing we did not complete and ignoring all the great things that we accomplished, negating our achievements. The result of doing this exercise is that you validate yourself more and focus on all that you did get accomplished.

1. _____

2. _____

3. _____

4. _____

5. _____

6. _____

7. _____

8. _____

9. _____

10. _____

Surround yourself with positive, supportive people

On the days when things in your life are not going so well, surrounding yourself with positive people will keep you focused and moving forward.

You must be willing to invest in yourself and your future if you want to be successful.

Enroll in that course you've always wanted to take. Sign up for those piano classes you've not thought about since you were eight years old. Join a networking organization, or get the coaching support you know will help boost your confidence and support your climb up the ladder of success and fulfillment. Just DO something to invest in your own state of well-being.

Manage your commitments, not your time

Do you wish you had more time? Well, you can have more time. When I tell my clients that they are the pilots and they do have the power to change, they look at me as if I'm speaking a foreign language. Yes, we can be our worst enemies. We shoot ourselves in the foot on a regular basis.

Everybody gets the same amount of hours in every day. That's not the problem. The problem is what you are doing with those 24 hours. Time management is a great tool to use as a way to become more efficient at handling tasks. It is *not* a great thing when you use it to beat yourself up because you can't get everything done. There's nothing wrong with you if you can't complete EVERYTHING you want to get done in a single 24 hours! You're just overcommitted. You say *yes* more times than you say *no*.

Stop worrying about managing time and start managing your commitments. When you manage your commitments, you are not as likely to get sidetracked by the bright shiny object syndrome. Set your intentions for the day so that you are clear about where you are going and what you want to get done.

Think before you commit. How many times do you say yes to others and five minutes later wished you would have said no? In all probability you realized that you weren't clear about the expectations and you bit off more than you could chew. This leads to guilt, resentment, and being out of integrity with yourself. Stop and check in with yourself before you commit to doing something for someone else.

Leave room for breakdowns. Stuff happens. It only becomes a problem when we let it ruin our whole day. Handle the breakdown and get back to where you were going in the first place.

The object of the game is not to fill up your day and just become more of a workaholic. Your work is to fill your day with tasks that are in keeping with your intentions, your core values, and what matters most to you in your personal and professional life. When you start managing your life out of your commitments, your life is permeated with more peace, passion, purpose, and productivity, with less overwhelm and more results.

Take time to celebrate yourself and all you bring to the table of life. Many of us have a hard time celebrating ourselves— tooting our own horns, so to speak. Action Exercise 17 is a powerful one—if you take it seriously.

▶ *Action Exercise 17*
100 WAYS TO CELEBRATE YOURSELF

Make a list of 100 things you love about you and celebrate them. For example, "I am a good parent; I am a good cook; I am a good friend; I am a great boss." The list goes on. Every time you get down on yourself, you can pull out that list and read what a fabulous person you are to jumpstart those good vibrations again.

It may take a while to come up with 100 items, but every time you think of one thing you're good at, put it on your list until you get to 100. Start today to make a list of 100 things to celebrate yourself!

Never give up on yourself and...the power of your dreams. Believe!

It is really easy to get sucked into believing an overnight success story, but what those stories are missing is that it took that person many years and a lot of hard work to get to first base. We live in what I call the *McDonald's Society*. We want it quick, easy, and good. However, what happens is that we become very impatient with our quest for success and we give up way too soon.

Let me give you an example. Remember when I mentioned earlier that in an effort to become healthier and gain muscular strength, I joined a local Pilates club? OMG! Talk about a workout, but I absolutely love it. The whole premise behind the class is doing the exercises very, very slowly to get the maximum results. My instructor is a sweetheart and excellent teacher. Her favorite words are, "Creep it, creep it. Tell those stomach muscles to do their job and don't quit." Now I know you have an 8 x10 glossy mental picture of me sweating, straining, and trembling to keep going and not give up. Believe me, in the early stages it was not a pretty picture, but I persevered and *that's* the important thing.

Whether it is in Pilates or in life, intentionality is very important to your success. The intention behind going slowly is that you concentrate on doing the exercise correctly to get the maximum results out of your efforts. In addition, you also find out what actions work and what actions don't work for you, hence you reach your goals faster.

Who would have thought that a success lesson would come from a Pilates class? Every time the instructor says, "Don't quit" it reminds me of how many times I have become impatient or given up because I wanted results right now. Whether it is in your business or your life, the same principles apply. In order to reach your goals, you must remember three things: patience, consistency, and commitment.

Patience—Since patience has never been one of my strong suits, this is a virtue that I continue to work on. The thing that you have to remember is that you didn't get the way you are overnight and you're not going to change it overnight. Stay the course.

Consistency—Whether it is a personal or a professional goal, you can't just do something once and expect it to magically transform you. You've got to keep working those muscles, whether it is a mental confidence muscle or a stomach muscle.

Commitment—The right mindset is everything. The key to success is to keep your vision of what you want in front of you at all times. It must be your goal, not something you think you should do because everybody else is doing it.

Success comes to those who are willing to work for it, however long it takes. If it is worth having, it's worth working for.

And, last but not the least, lighten up! Laughter is still the best medicine. Life is really not that hard. We just make it seem that way. Sometimes all we need to brighten up our day is a good belly laugh. Call one of your best friends and go have an ice cream cone, and while you're eating it, pretend you're 10 again.

Well, there you have it. These strategies keep me grounded,

focused, and moving in the right direction every day of my life. With regular practice, I'm positive that they will work for you, too.

NINE DO'S AND DONT'S OF SUCCESSFUL PEOPLE

"The way to get started is to quit talking and begin doing."

~ Walt Disney

I was recently talking with one of my clients who had taken a giant leap of faith in her business which, when implemented, was going to catapult her company to great success. I was so proud of her because she had chosen to invest in herself and her ultimate success. When I asked how she felt, she said, "Scared to death," but she knew it was time to quit talking about success and take action. It was time to go big or go home and she wasn't going home. She could no longer sit on the sidelines waiting for fate to take its course.

This conversation reminded me of my own cathartic moment when my coach asked me if my business was a serious endeavor or just a hobby. Talk about a wake up call. But then that's why you hire a coach—to ask you the hard questions that you haven't thought of or don't want to face. That was a turning point for me. That is when I started taking myself and my business much more seriously.

Don't get me wrong, I love helping people achieve their goals, but I wanted to reach out and help as many as possible to be the best that they can be, and you can't do that by thinking small and playing safe.

If your intention is to be successful, then you are going to have to take the actions that successful people take. Successful people don't just talk about their goals, they take concrete steps to get them there.

Successful people DON'T...

- ...wait for the right time. If you wait, the right time might never come along.

- ...hesitate if an opportunity presents itself. They seize the opportunity and run with it.

- ...ask the price before they look at value. They know that they need to invest in their business and themselves because both endeavors are worth it.

- ...let fear stop them. They face fear straight on, decide a clear path, and then plow through those roadblocks.

- ...wait for someone else to make the first move. Exactly "who" is that someone going to be if it isn't you, the business owner?

- ...worry about making a mistake. Making mistakes is how we grow and learn new techniques to help our businesses thrive.

- ...let the "yeah, buts" get in their way. The word *but* is just another pothole on the pathway to success that you need to avoid while continuing your journey.

- ...associate with negative people. Always associate with positive people who support you and your vision. Negativity breeds more negativity. Who needs that in their life?

- ...don't whine or make excuses about why they are not successful. You can be a victim or a victor. Choose to be a victor and be successful.

Successful people DO...

- ...take action. They make a decision, a strategic plan, and then they implement it.

- ...make things happen. Set the wheels in motion to take that leap of faith and just do it.

- ...seize opportunities. Investigate that new idea you have for growing your business and then turn that idea into a reality.

- ..learn the skills they need to succeed. By investing in yourself, you're investing in your business—a win-win situation.

- ...become fearless. Whenever fear rears its ugly head, stare it straight in the eye and say, "You have no place in my business or my life. I WILL SUCCEED!"

- ...know that there are no mistakes, just learning opportunities. As an old friend of mine used to say back in the Dark Ages, "Mistakes are why erasers were invented." Use that same philosophy when it comes to conquering your fear of making a blunder in your business.

- ...surround themselves with positive, supportive people. By surrounding yourself with people who are where you want to be, you double or triple the chances of succeeding.

- ...get support. Never be afraid to reach out and ask someone to help you. If you need additional team members, hire them. If you need a coach or mentor to help you clarify your direction and offer new perspective, then find one.

- ...expect to succeed with unwavering faith. They never settle for less than what they truly want in their business or their lives.

So, what about you? Are you doing the things that successful people do to get what you want or are you going to settle for playing small? Is your life or business what you want it to be or do your feet feel like they're encased in concrete? Are you merely talking about instituting changes or taking firm actions to get to where you want to go?

It's your decision. Choose wisely.

STEP SEVEN:
CARVE OUT "ME TIME" REGULARLY

"For even when the time comes and you can relax,
you hardly know how."

– Alice Foote MacDougall

Ah, I've been saving the most delicious bites of wisdom for last! Compassionate self-care. They say we teach that which we need to learn, and believe me, this has been the work of all works for me. The pull is so strong to fall back into my own people-pleaser ways that I have to maintain a constant vigilance to ensure that I don't return.

Isn't it fascinating that we invest in everything from the stock market, to our children, our friends, our careers, but not in ourselves? I was one of those women who gave and gave until one day I woke up and realized I had nothing left to give. I was all used up. I had been on autopilot for so long that when the time came to relax and do something for me, I hardly knew how. For most of us, carving out *me time* regularly is a pretty radical idea.

One of the most common complaints that my clients have when they come to me is they want more balance and less stress in their lives. The sad part about it is that they have no clue how to achieve this feat. The first thing they tell me is, "I don't have time." The reason they don't have time is that they are too busy taking care of everything and everybody else but themselves. Remember, you are preaching to the choir here. All the excuses you can give, I've used them myself. If you don't take time out for yourself now, you will become resentful and resigned, and the stress will physically start taking its toll on your body. There are only 24 hours in a day and those hours contain 86,400 seconds. Surely you can find a few of these seconds to take care of you.

Some of you may be saying to yourself, "I do take time out for me" and if that is the case with you, I acknowledge and congratulate you for your efforts. But for some, giving yourself permission and making the request is a lot more difficult.

If, however, you fall into the category of not taking time for yourself or you feel guilty when you do take time for yourself, then there are action steps that you can take to change it.

Plan your "me time"

Having *me time* is not going to happen until you plan for it. You plan the rest of your life; why not plan time for you? Believe me, I know from where I speak. I have been a single parent for most of my life and it did take a whole lot of planning to carve out some *me time* when my children were young.

If carving out time for yourself is something that is new for you, start small, and then work your way up. To help get you started, I've included Action Exercise 18 for you to kick start your efforts to making time for yourself daily.

▶ *Action Exercise 18*
CARVING OUT "ME TIME"

Decide how much time a week you want to dedicate to your *me time*. For example, one hour a week, one evening out, etc. The length of your *me time* is irrelevant at first—just get into the routine of setting aside an amount of time that is solely dedicated to doing what *you* want.

Determine what free-time activities would appeal to you. Here are some suggestions to inspire you to think of what you would really enjoy doing.

◆ Thirty minute walk by yourself

◆ Get out for a round of golf

◆ Reading a few chapters in a good book

- Hit the gym for a workout

- Go to a movie by yourself or with friends

- Enjoy dinner out for a change

Choose whatever appeals to you. After all, this is *your* special time; just pick one idea and do it. Choose one activity and plan your schedule accordingly to make it happen. No excuses!

Do it! Keep the commitment to yourself. Make the arrangements. Set up the babysitter. Have a conversation with your spouse, or ask a friend to keep you accountable when you start to wimp out on yourself. *Do whatever it takes. Just make it happen.*

You've got a plan. Now what?
Dealing with the guilt trip that is sure to come

For most of us, making a plan is one thing, but following through is another. Sure as I'm sitting here someone is going to want to throw a monkey wrench into your plan, whether it is your children, your honey, your boss, your friends, yada, yada, yada. In other words, they are going to try to put a guilt trip on you.

When my children were younger and I wanted to go out, my mother would call me just to ask me if I was sure I wanted to leave my children home with a babysitter. And then went on to tell me that I really needed to stay home. My mother was from the old school and single women weren't supposed to go out without an escort. Keep in mind that I was a widow at the time. The way I would handle it was just to say, "That won't work for me, Mom." It took me a lot of practice to be able to say that. However, I knew in my heart of hearts that that was what I needed to do to take care of me.

So, what's the point to this story? It's this—there will always be naysayers in your life. Here's what I want you to remember when they make negative comments. *It is not about you!* It is about them and their wish to control you! *Your* work is to stand tall in your power and your dignity, determine what works for you, and go with it.

Don't give away your power. Ever!

Once you've mastered the one hour or one evening out regularly and are really enjoying the new found time for yourself, I have another radical self care idea for you.

A weekend retreat or getaway just for YOU. Alone!

Wow! I know. I thought it was pretty radical too when my coach first mentioned it, but the more I thought about it, the more I liked the idea. I have been single for a lot of years, so being by myself is nothing new. However, it's not the same as uninterrupted quiet time with no phones, no computer, no schedule, no TV, no outside influences, and no chatter. Going off by myself to the beach is one of the best things that I do to rest, recharge, and renew myself.

Think about this. We take in over 15,000 messages a day. Your mind is always on *go* whether you think it is or not. So, how are you going to think about what you want and where you are going if you don't take quiet time to just *be*?

If you are going to be up to creating big things in the world, then you are going to have to take care of yourself first.

I now know that the better I take care of myself physically, emotionally, and spiritually, the more I have to give to others. I am definitely more peaceful, more productive, more joyful, and definitely more powerful.

I am worth it, and so are you!

SELF PRESERVATION DOES NOT EQUAL SELF-CARE

"Until you value yourself you will not value your time.
Until you value your time, you will not do anything with it."

– M. Scott Peck

In a recent survey I conducted, I was surprised that when asked to choose some of the challenges they face in life and business, a lot of respondents checked self-care. Matter of fact, one respondent asked me the question, "What *is* self-care?" I was so taken aback because I thought everyone was clear on what that term meant.

Self-care is what I have struggled with for the last 15 plus years—actually, all of my life—but I was so unconscious the first half of my life that I didn't have a clue until my coach started asking me questions I couldn't answer. I used to live in fear that he would ask me how I was feeling or what my mood was. Why? Because I was like a wind-up doll. Wind me up, point me in the right direction, and I did what I was expected to do. On the outside, everything seemed just peachy; but on the inside I was dying. I was burned out and there was a hole in my soul; something vital was missing.

I know I talk a lot about building up your levels of self-confidence and self-esteem, learning to set boundaries, and saying no to requests that rob you of not only your time but your integrity, but what does the art of self-care really encompass? Certainly self-care includes taking the best possible care of our personal health and living in the healthiest manner possible, but what about our interior health? You know—the one we sometimes fear to examine too closely, namely our mental and spiritual well-being? Anyone can pop a vitamin pill, but how do you change areas in your thinking (mindset) that are constantly sabotaging your business and life?

You can keep burying your problems (and your head) in the sand, all the while telling yourself that they don't exist, but sooner or later I can guarantee you that those difficulties you're struggling with are going to rear their ugly heads and bite you in the butt. Hiding out behind that nice-person, do-as-you're-told role in the hopes that no one will find out your secret will only last so long. Trust me. Trying to keep up that facade will catch up with you.

So, what happens when you finally get found out, like I did? All the little things that never bothered you before start getting to you. You find yourself becoming resigned and resentful. You may think you're practicing self-preservation and doing fairly well at it. However, at some point you're going to have to stop and take a look in the mirror at the person who is staring back at you. Otherwise, you will wind up living someone else's life like I was, instead of the life you truly want deep down in your soul.

What I can tell you is that this phenomenon is not terminal. I am living proof that you can learn how to take care of yourself at any age. You can change if you are willing to do your work and get the support you need. You can stop settling and start living life on your terms.

Here are some of the steps that I used to reclaim the pieces of myself that I had given away in my life like my dignity, integrity, courage, and self-esteem.

◆ **Define what's working and not working in your life.** Make a list. You're going to want to have a starting point from which to start living your most authentic life.

◆ **Make a list of the three changes you want to make in the next 90 days.** Be realistic in your choices of changes. If you want to lose 40 pounds, don't make it your goal to get there in 30 days or you'll end up in the hospital from malnutrition.

◆ **Start small and build up to the biggies** as your confidence grows. If your goal is to start saying no to others to regain your time, start off with a little no.

◆ **Let go of what you are not willing to change at the present time.** Don't beat yourself up! There are lots of negative people out in the world that can do that for you without you having to be your own worst enemy.

◆ **Invest in yourself.** I know that I would not be where I am today had I not gotten the coaching and mentoring support I needed. You can do it on your own, but you don't have to.

Success starts with self care. It is the foundation that turns an ordinary life into an extraordinary life. And who among us wants to go through life merely existing instead of living a rich, juicy, and passion-filled life? Not me.

CONCLUSION

"Success can make you go one of two ways.
It can make you a prima donna, or it can smooth the edges,
take away the insecurities, let the nice things come out."

– *Barbara Walters*

Let's face it. You didn't get this book just because you felt like spending your money, did you? At least I hope not. No, you got it because you were sick and tired of trying to fit into other people's expectations of who you should and should not be. You were tired of second guessing yourself, tired of using strategies that no longer worked for you, and tired of not getting the results you wanted and deserved. You wanted more time, more success, more confidence, with less stress in your life, and I don't blame you one bit. I acknowledge you for recognizing that you do have a choice about how you live your life and for not giving up on yourself.

As you have moved through the steps and done the Action Exercises, you have learned seven powerful strategies.

◆ Define what success means to you.

◆ Use your core values to make all your decisions.

◆ Begin to set boundaries.

◆ Say what you mean and mean what you say.

◆ Master the art of presenting ideas and handling difficult conversations.

◆ Plan to succeed daily.

◆ Carve out *me time* regularly.

With these seven strategies you can now climb the ladder of success without having to struggle so hard all the time. These tactics will help you stay one step ahead of competition and always be at the top of your game. Success is really not that difficult when you have the right tools. As human beings, we just make it hard. I know. I did exactly that for years.

Will this system work for you? That depends on the degree of your commitment to the change process. I don't have any magic pill that will make your life all better. Nor do I have any special pixie dust to sprinkle on you to make all your problems fade away. *You* will still need to do your portion of the work. What I can tell you is that when you implement these strategies, you begin to create more realistic expectations of yourself and others, and eliminate unnecessary second guessing that can keep you stuck. You will feel calmer, more in control, and enjoy even more success in your business and your personal life.

Will you still have breakdowns and make mistakes? Yes, you will, but you will handle them, learn from them, and move forward a lot faster than you did before. That being said, even if you implement only one action step, it will make an immediate difference in your life. I guarantee it.

Here's what I know for sure will happen when you implement the strategies I've shared with you in this book:

◆ Improve your ability to lead and delegate

◆ Identify big visions

◆ Make sound decisions quickly and efficiently

◆ Bridge the gap between your goals and your actions

◆ Ignite productivity and effectiveness

◆ Build negotiating skills and manage conflicts more effectively

◆ Develop a heightened sense of confidence

◆ Coordinate action more effectively

◆ Stay calm and focused when under pressure

◆ Create more of what you do want and less of what you don't want in your life personally and professionally

◆ Have more time off to enjoy the fruits of your successes

◆ Have more *gioia-di-vivere*! (that means "joy of living" in Italian)

It is said that the journey to success begins with one step. So I challenge you to climb up on that ladder, and take that first step today.

ABOUT THE AUTHOR

"My expertise helps people find within themselves the tools and skills they need to be successful..... to grow and achieve beyond their wildest dreams."

Cookie Tuminello

As founder and CEO of the top coaching and consulting firm Success Source, Cookie seasons her powerful leadership and team development programs with a unique and entertaining style that combines humor and humanity. She is an accomplished author, mega-motivational speaker and stellar leadership and team development coach. Her clients include CEOs, managers, business owners and organizational leaders who want to get results now. Built on solid business practices, Cookie offers leadership and personnel training that helps you and your team cut to the chase, stop wasting time, and tackle issues head on—ultimately, creating a healthier bottom line. Get powerful results: *http://www.CookieTuminello.com*.

LEARN MORE

Cookie offers a variety of learning and teaching opportunities through her website:

www.CookieTuminello.com

We invite you to sign up for Cookie's free weekly ezine, *Coffee With Cookie*, for tips, tools and strategies that will inspire and motivate you to grow, succeed, and create that competitive edge in the marketplace. When you join, you will also receive my free report, *101 Keys to Unlocking Your Power and Potential*.

This publication is free of charge and is our way of supporting the growing number of leaders who want to build solid business practices that create long-term, measurable results and stay a step ahead of the competition. To get your free subscription, visit www.CookieTuminello.com.

SEMINARS AND WORKSHOPS

Cookie provides national and international workshops, seminars, and keynote speeches on the topics of leadership, communication, self-confidence, human capital management, infrastructure development, as well as creating vision-oriented teams that embrace change and growth. For smaller groups, entrepreneurs, and executives, she offers *Refocus and Restore* retreats several times during the year.